# SEASONS *for* TROUT

# SEASONS *for* TROUT

Rick Hafele
Dave Hughes
Skip Morris

STACKPOLE
BOOKS

Published by
STACKPOLE BOOKS
5067 Ritter Road
Mechanicsburg, PA 17055
www.stackpolebooks.com

Printed in China

10 9 8 7 6 5 4 3 2 1

FIRST EDITION

Cover design by Caroline M. Stover
Cover photo by Rick Hafele
All flies in Skip Morris's chapters tied by the author.

**Library of Congress Cataloging-in-Publication Data**

Hafele, Rick.
  Seasons for trout / Rick Hafele, Dave Hughes, and Skip Morris.
    pages cm
  ISBN 978-0-8117-1340-5
  1. Trout fishing.  I. Hughes, Dave, 1945- II. Morris, Skip. III. Title.
  SH687.H24 2014
  799.17'57—dc23
                        2014003131

# Contents

# Acknowledgments

I want to thank all the readers of *HookedNow* who sent us their support and encouragement to keep writing it for the two and half years of its life. I also want to thank Judith Schnell of Stackpole for believing in this book, and Brittany Stoner for all her efforts to bring this material together and coordinate with three authors at once—no small task.

*—Rick Hafele*

I'd like to thank Rick and Skip for the fun we had fishing together, "researching" the stories that became this book.

*—Dave Hughes*

Every chapter I've contributed here is stuffed tight with ideas I learned mostly from others over a lifetime of fly fishing. How could I possibly thank them all (if I could actually remember them all) without filling this book with unnecessary pages you shouldn't have to pay for? So, to those who taught me so much, thanks everyone!

But a few contributed directly and recently, and since they *are* only a few, I want to thank the following fine people: my beloved wife, Carol Ann Morris, for her many vivid and instructive photographs and for her help in selecting the best ones for each chapter; my dear old pal Rick Hafele for guiding this whole project from the start and for all the time he devoted to editing the videos; Judith Schnell for believing in and organizing our three-man books and Brittany Stoner for getting the details correct; and Dave Hughes for his valuable perspective along the way and just for being a longtime and cherished friend.

*—Skip Morris*

# Introduction

Rick Hafele, Dave Hughes, and Skip Morris are three guys who love to fish with flies. They love it so much that they've found ways to devote a lot of their lives, their time, their work, and their play to fly fishing.

Rick is trained as an aquatic entomologist and knows hatches better than trout do. Dave leads any list of bright, accomplished fly-fishing authors. Skip's specialty is fly tying, and his books and videos get beginners tying handsome, effective flies and help more experienced tiers improve. The three are well known and highly regarded in the fly-fishing world. They've written scores of books, done instructional videos, and been published hundreds of times in the best fly-fishing magazines. They are sought out as speakers for fly-fishing clubs, sportsmen's shows, and conclaves. They are fly-fishing stars.

But writing about fishing, or speaking about fishing, or peering through camera lenses and microscopes at the aquatic insects that fish feed on . . . well, that isn't fishing. They weren't getting enough time out on streams. Sound familiar? What to do?

They dreamed up the idea of going off on fishing trips together and writing about it, each from his own perspective, and then publishing the info in an e-magazine. They started *HookedNow*, signed up five hundred subscribers, took those trips, had the fun that they had missed, and then worked very hard writing, photographing, making videos, and publishing the magazine for two years. But soon enough the work part of the dream took over, and they were back where they didn't want to be: doing a lot of work and not enough fishing.

That's where I enter the picture. My advice to them: You three go fishing, I'll do the publishing. And now, with this book, you have the result.

I've known these three for a long time. I met up with them twenty-five years ago on—you guessed it—a fishing trip. I was in Portland visiting Dave Hughes so we could talk about book ideas. Dave and I had published a few titles by then and, as his editor at Stackpole, I wanted more. We talked books—as we have over the many years since—and came up with years' worth of work for both of us. For a break from all the talk, Dave thought it would be fun for us to go fishing. He organized a trip on the Willamette River for me and his best friends, among them Rick and Skip. They fished. I watched. I was surrounded by talent. It was an intimidatingly accomplished group and I wasn't ready to show my ineptitude. (It took me a good long while to catch the fly-fishing bug.) But, no question, that float trip and watching these guys playfully try to outfish each other was fun. Such expertise, such camaraderie. As you dip into the pages of this book, you'll see.

*Seasons for Trout*, and its companion book *Tactics for Trout*, are as new and innovative a presentation of collective fishing wit and wisdom as this year's hot new fly. The books are a collaborative effort all the way—each of the guys writes in his own voice, from his own perspective, bringing insights and experience to the task at hand: going fishing and catching trout. It's a collaboration of three very talented, knowledgeable, and likeable fishing buddies.

Combining another trio—text, photos, and videos—within a print book is a winning format. With QR codes throughout, you're able to watch and learn from on-stream videos, very much as if you were there with the three guys themselves. And the enhanced ebook version of the book is also an impressive way to read it.

A winning format, a winning trio of authors. Go fishing with Rick, Dave, and Skip, and have fun!

—*Judith Schnell*,
Publisher

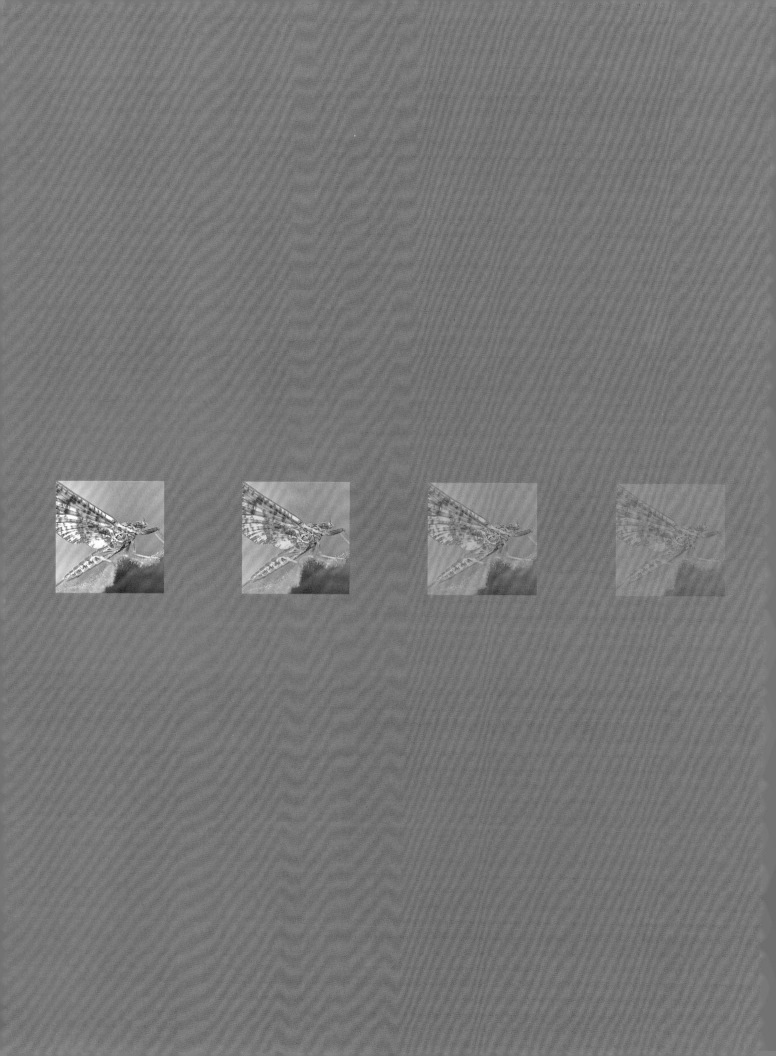

# Spring

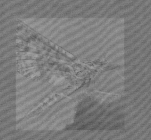   

Is it spring yet? Don't be fooled by the calendar—
the bugs will tell you when spring has arrived.
RICK HAFELE

*Rick Hafele*

# My Favorite Spring Hatch

W hen exactly spring starts can be tricky to say. Of course the calendar does give us an exact time: This year the vernal equinox (start of spring) was at 7:02 a.m. on March 20. However, you might have a different opinion about the start of spring if you happen to live where a big snowstorm arrived on or after that date. I find it's safer to go by all the signals we get from nature, like when trilliums burst out on the forest floor, when crocuses pop up in gardens and yards, and when trees sprout bright green new leaves, not to mention all the activity by the birds and the bees. Nature also tells us when spring has arrived on streams and lakes. In fact, for fly fishers spring provides a lot more to look forward to than just daffodils in the garden. The first hatches of the year can be some of the best of the year, and that's what I want to discuss in this chapter—one of my favorite spring hatches.

Western March Browns begin emerging before the cottonwoods have leafed out on the Willamette River in Oregon.
RICK HAFELE

## March Browns

It's difficult to pick a favorite spring hatch, but over the years March Browns have provided enough memories that their hatch always seems to mark the beginning of a new fishing season. The Western March Brown, a.k.a. *Rhithrogena morrisoni*, is a clinger mayfly widely distributed throughout the West. There are mayflies that hatch earlier than *R. morrisoni*, namely species of *Baetis* or Blue-Winged Olives, but when it comes to signals of spring *R. morrisoni* seems to trigger that "winter is finally over" feeling. The start of this hatch, like any other, is weather dependent. Its name clearly suggests that March is the month you'll find it, and in many years

that's exactly the case. When winter weather lingers well into March, however, the hatch becomes much more the Western April Brown, and in some mild winters it would best be called the Western February Brown. In most years, though, you will find mid-March to mid-April the period when Western March Browns grace many Western streams with a good dose of dry fly fishing.

If you live in the Midwestern or Eastern part of the country you will still find March Browns, but they will be the American March Brown, *Stenonema vicarium*, rather than *R. morrisoni*. *S. vicarium* also belongs to the clinger group of mayflies, and just as spring often comes later to the Midwest and East, *S. vicarium* hatches typically run from mid-May to late June.

start of dun emergence. This is a midday hatch, typically 1:00 to 3:00, depending on the specific weather on the day you're fishing—warmer days mean earlier emergence by an hour or two and colder days a later emergence by an hour or so. Also cloudy, even slightly wet, days will almost always produce better hatch activity than clear, sunny days.

For fishing nymphs, I go with a standard approach: a weighted nymph, a split shot on the leader 8 to 10 inches up from the fly, and a strike indicator located about twice the depth of the water from the fly. Don't be tempted to use a bigger nymph pattern than the naturals, as you will catch more fish

A *Rhithrogena morrisoni* nymph and its imitation. I worry less about color and more about size when picking a pattern for either nymphs or duns. DAVE HUGHES (TOP); RICK HAFELE (BOTTOM)

As clingers, March Brown nymphs are lovers of medium to fast water where the bottom is composed of softball- to bowling-ball-size rocks. To get a good idea of when the hatch may start, collect some nymphs off the rocks and look closely at their wing pads. If the wing pads are dark brown to almost black, then the hatch is imminent. If you don't see any nymphs with dark wing pads, you can safely assume you have another couple weeks to wait before duns will start popping out on the surface. Water temperature can also be a guide. For the Western March Brown, water temperatures of around 46 or 47 degrees generally trigger the beginning of hatch activity.

When you find some mature nymphs but the hatch has yet to start, it can be a great time to fish nymph imitations. Once the hatch has started, fishing nymph patterns is still effective prior to the actual

Try nymphing in choppy riffles from mid-morning to early afternoon, before the duns start appearing later in the day.
RICK HAFELE

with a nymph pattern of the proper size. Sometimes this seems counterintuitive as the larger fly would seem to be easier for fish to see, especially if spring streamflows are up and slightly off color, but trout seem to have exceptional vision and are often picky eaters, even for nymphs. For all my fishing, I find size more important than color when it comes to catching selective trout.

Of course when you're looking forward to fishing a good hatch, fishing nymphs is not your primary goal. Once a few duns start popping up on the surface, I like to put on a dry fly and add a nymph 18 to 20 inches below it with a piece of tippet attached to the bend of the dry fly's hook. This way you can see if the fish are more interested in the nymphs rising to the surface or the duns floating on top. If fish are rising but ignoring your dry fly, then it's time to put on an emerger pattern. One I've frequently used for March Browns is a soft-hackled pattern or March Brown Flymph. Fish it dead-drift right over rising

trout, and if you get no takers, let it swing in the current at the tail end of the drift. When fishing drys, pay attention to drag. The trout may be hungry and eager in the spring, but they still get put off by a dragging dry fly.

Like most days on a stream, it's impossible to predict exactly what's going to happen, and that's certainly true of spring fishing. On more than one occasion, I've started a day's float trip down the Willamette River, one of my favorite local streams for the March Brown hatch, in what appears to be perfect conditions—overcast sky, little wind, and mild temperature—only to have the weather change swiftly a couple hours later with rapidly dropping temperature followed by rain and wind. On these days, I am lucky to take even a few fish on nymphs. On the best days, the weather cooperates, the clouds hang in the sky like a soft blanket, and a light breeze carries the scent of new cottonwood leaves. Then, just about the time we pull over to eat lunch on a warm gravel bar below

a gentle riffle, the first duns start popping up on the surface, and the first swallows start twisting down from above to take them with quick snaps of their beaks. More duns quickly follow, and then the first rise of a trout breaks the surface. It's hard to explain the feeling I get when that first rise is seen during the first March Brown hatch of the year, but it's when I know spring has arrived.

As we all know, however, the abundance of spring doesn't stop with the March Brown hatch. Numerous other insects also let swallows, trout, and anglers know that spring has arrived. You will find detailed information about two of these, the *Skwala* stonefly and *Glossosoma* caddisfly, in other parts of this section. And yet spring provides even more. There's the spring hatch of mahogany duns—the mayfly family Leptophlebiidae and genus *Paraleptophlebia*—and the ubiquitous but tiny Blue-Winged Olives and midges. Eastern and Midwestern waters also see a variety of early season mayfly hatches like the Slate-Winged Mahogany Dun (*Paraleptophlebia*) and Quill Gordon (*Epeorus pleuralis*), to name just a couple. In lakes, the *Callibaetis* mayfly provides excellent early season action, and the early spring chironomid hatches offer some of the best lake fishing of the year. To me, this abundance of new life is what makes spring fishing so fascinating and enjoyable, and at times challenging. The challenge is all part of the fun however, so no matter what you find trout rising to on your next spring fishing trip, take some time to just sit back and appreciate the abundance of a new season.

The March Brown dun is just one stage you'll need to match during a hatch. It's good to have a selection of fly patterns that cover all stages: nymphs, emergers, duns, and spinners. Bottom row: Peacock Herl Nymph; MB Nymph. Middle row: CDC Parachute Emerger; MB Flymph. Top row: Harrop Hairwing Dun; Rusty Spinner. DAVE HUGHES (TOP); RICK HAFELE (BOTTOM)

Jim Schollmeyer fishing a streamer in early spring water on Oregon's Owyhee River, famous for its big brown trout. DAVE HUGHES

*Dave Hughes*

# Spring Tactics

Spring tactics depend entirely on the spring situation, and you've noticed as well as I have that conditions vary across as wide a range in spring as in all the other seasons added together. You've got to be prepared to fish anything from a tiny midge or BWO mayfly hatch on smooth water to nymphs and streamers deep in water that is blown out. Rather than describe tactics specific to each condition, I'll give some examples of problems and solutions in my own fishing from recent springs.

# Dave Hughes

The most dramatic came on a scheduled float of the Deschutes River with Curt Marr. He has a tighter calendar than mine. When he plans a trip, he's reluctant to miss it. Rain piled up in the days before our dates; reservoirs got full; and water was released. The day we were to leave, levels were at 9500 cfs, twice what they ought to be for the best Deschutes fishing. I called Curt to see if he might not want to cancel.

He said, "Let's go. At least we'll have a float."

We had a float. When we put his raft in at Trout Creek, the water was at the promised height and approached the color of skim milk . . . not quite that white, but more chalky than clear. Things looked pretty hopeless for entertaining any trout.

Late in the afternoon of the first day on the river, Curt said, "Since we aren't going to catch any trout, how about showing me how you would rig to fish nymphs in these kinds of conditions." I was reluctant, but I did. I rigged a 10-foot leader with a big bubble indicator up top, 6 or 8 feet of leader down to a couple of heavy split shot, a big Salmonfly nymph 10 inches below the shot, and a size 16 Lightning Bug on point 8 inches from the larger nymph. We parked the boat in a backchannel behind an island where the current was a bit broken, not nearly as deep as the main current I would fish in normal conditions . . . had I gotten into that water I'd have instantly been swept away.

I made some demonstration casts, lobbing them far upstream to give the heavy outfit plenty of time to sink and then mending and tending the line to keep the indicator floating freely, just as you'd do in more

---

**Below:** Curt Marr fishing the kind of water that forms fine trout lies when the water on the Deschutes is twice too high and trout move into places where the current is broken, in this case by a stump that would not even be in the water when the water is at normal height. He took half a dozen nice trout on nymphs from this line of lies.
DAVE HUGHES

Another example of a spot that would not even be one when the water is at normal elevation. The slight backeddy to which Curt Marr is casting gave trout shelter from the surge of high flows, and he caught a couple of trout. DAVE HUGHES

**Right:** It seems that trout in high and cloudy water would be tucked into sheltered lies and not feeding, but this throat-pump sample is evidence that trout on the Deschutes River find lots of large groceries dislodged and available in high water. DAVE HUGHES

reasonable water. I got the bugs worked out of the presentation; the bobber bounced along, hesitating once in a while to let me know the shot nicked the bottom now and then. Things were going smoothly, in terms of showing Curt what I'd do if I had any hope of catching trout. Of course it was not long before I hung up and prepared to make the part in the demonstration about losing everything and having to re-rig every few minutes. When I tugged at the

snag in hopes of freeing whatever had got lodged, whatever it was tugged back and then suddenly shot downstream.

You know the rest of the story. It turned out the trout had done the same thing Curt and I did: They found a soft spot in the current, on the backside of an island, to idle away their time until the water became more reasonable out where they'd rather be. That first animated snag turned out to be the most

# Dave Hughes

aggressive trout in a pod of them. We were able to educate half a dozen about the perils of bottom-bounced nymphs before fishing dried up there, and we trotted off downstream.

It was a three-day float. We camped, suffered heavy rain, didn't get to see the water subside even an inch, clear up even a bit, but were able to find three or four isolated pods of trout each day. We took several trout from each pod before moving on. It became far more of a challenge to read the water right and find the trout than it did to rig right and catch the trout. They were in the kinds of places that wouldn't be places when the water was normal. Every one of these holding areas was defined by something that broke the current, whether it was the point of an island deflecting it outward, the bouldered bottom of a riffle causing hidden soft spots, or the root wad of a tree that would in normal circumstances have been safely up on shore. Wherever the current hesitated, we found a few trout.

A perfect description of the most common holding lies, in that high water, would be the kinds of side riffles that would normally be just a foot deep, too shallow to hold trout, and that you'd pass by on a normal float. Perhaps you've noticed those tiny rippled spots, always on the inside bends in the river, and like me, you've likely tried fishing a few of them in your past and always found them fishless. They always look good, but trout are usually busy holding in water that offers them more protection from osprey and otter . . . and us. But when the water is high and off-color, trout don't need that protection. What they need is shelter from the brisk currents. They find it in all those spots that would not be spots if the water was lower.

Jim Schollmeyer and I stopped at the Owyhee River in Oregon last spring on our way to the Bighorn

---

**Below:** Curt Marr fishing the inside edge of an island on the Deschutes River, where trout had tucked themselves in to avoid the high and heavy current. DAVE HUGHES

Jim Schollmeyer on Oregon's Owyhee River, fishing streamers to lies that are invisible in the high and slightly cloudy water and that therefore must be found with your flies. DAVE HUGHES

in Montana. The water was a bit high and slightly off-color when we got there. A constant supply of rain while we were there did not serve to cause the water to drop and clear, which is what we wanted it to do. We hoped to fish hatches of midges and BWOs, with those big browns, for which the river is so famous, tipping up to sip them. We got none of that.

But we were able to get fair fishing simply by rigging with floating lines, 6- to 8-foot leaders, and streamers with some lead in their bellies. The water was extremely difficult to read because the river's flows are tamed by the dam upstream, and when it's opaque, you can't see into it to reveal the contours of its bottom. A shallow flat doesn't look much different from a submerged riffle; the current levels them both out. Boulder-garden runs stood out because you could see where the landscape alongside some runs tumbled boulders right into them, and you could also see the few boulders that protruded and slight boils sent up by others that were too deep to stick out. These places

held trout, and we were able to take a few from them, but they were also leg-breakers because it was impossible to see where to wade safely.

Most of our fishing was done by simply exploring with big streamers. We'd insert ourselves at the head of a long run of what looked like promising water, then cast long against the far bank, let those streamers sink, retrieve them back in fits and starts. Our project was to swim them through the places where the water dropped off, became suddenly deep, formed invisible lies for nice trout. It was reading water for soft spots, the same as Curt and I had done it on the Deschutes, only we didn't read the water with our eyes; we read it with our streamers. They found the deep spots for us. In turn, the deep spots provided a few trout for us.

It was interesting fishing until a monstrous thunderstorm blew us off the river. Rain landed in buckets, scathed the landscape, tumbled rocks off the steep hillsides, sent even ducks looking for shelter and

# Dave Hughes

quacking in protest. It soured our attitude and ended our fishing. We didn't stick around to see if the water came up and went even further off-color. We got out of there, and it's likely that you came about the time we left, arrived in sunshine, got to fish water that became low and clear, were able to present your dry flies to trout rising to sip those midges and BWOs.

Our destination was the Bighorn River, where we set up Jim's trailer at Cottonwood Camp. The weather there was closer to bitter, on the trailing edge of winter rather than the leading edge of spring. The water was normal, neither high nor off-color. But it was cold, and the hatches we hoped to fish hadn't started yet. We floated every day anyway and got into small pods of trout rising sporadically to scant numbers of a variety of things that trickled off: olives, midge pupae, scattered Early Brown stones, various things the trout tipped up to take but that we were never able to collect and observe. It was slow fishing.

I decided to practice some wet-fly swinging techniques I'd learned from Davy Wotton, the wet-fly

guru, while fishing with him on the White River in Arkansas. I'd bought an 11-foot rod and supple floating line in order to outfit for his high-rod method. Because rises were so sprinkled that I didn't feel compelled to cast over them, I sat in the grass at the edge of the river, next to Jim's boat, and patiently strung that long rod, fixed a 9-foot 5X leader, tied a Pheasant Tail Flashback to the tip, added 3 feet more of 5X, tied a Tungsten Bead Pheasant Tail to it as the point. The great Davy would have rigged with three wet flies in a variety of sizes, sink rates and colors, but I reckoned the trout must be seeing and taking at least a few BWO nymphs and wanted to imitate them for my own pleasure if not theirs.

It turned out the trout were quite pleased by this setup. I waded into a broad riffle that faded out into an even broader run, the kind the Bighorn features and that can take an hour or two to fish if trout are at all active. They were, in far greater numbers than showed on the surface. Just a few of them rose, on sparing occasions, the length of that entire stretch of

Woolly Buggers in black, olive, and brown are often the gold standard for trout holding in heavy and off-color water, but they need to have some weight to get down to the levels where big trout hold.
DAVE HUGHES

**Right:** It's good to arm yourself with a couple of nymphs when the water is high and off-color. An imitation of the Salmonfly nymph, in this case Charlie Brooks's Montana Stone, will help get you down to the bottom.
DAVE HUGHES

Jim Schollmeyer with a nice Owyhee brown trout that fell for a streamer fished deep on a slow swing. DAVE HUGHES

**Below:** Various versions of the famous Pheasant Tail Nymph that can be fished on the swing when the BWO hatch is about to begin. Be sure to kick around in the currents and collect a few naturals and make sure your fly is at least approximately the same size. DAVE HUGHES

# Dave Hughes

water. I didn't bother rushing to them, casting over them. Instead, I entered at the head of the riffle and then worked my way downstream as patiently as I would had I been covering it for summer steelhead or Atlantic salmon. I worked out a long line. The slow rod, with its construction of wide, open loops, didn't cause me any troubles, in the form of tangles.

When that brace of Pheasant Tails landed, always cutting across the currents at just a slight angle downstream, I'd give them a few feet to sink. Then I would make upstream mends to slow them, to swim them, I hoped, as patiently as BWO mayfly nymphs might rise from the bottom in that water that bordered on frigid.

Trout didn't hit with any thuds. Instead, they would intercept the nymphs gently, tug at them with great hesitation, or tap-tap them as you would expect from a steelhead. It was counterproductive to set the

**Below:** Guide Matt Granberg demonstrates the high rod and curved line technique that can be highly effective when trout feed on scattered nymphs active in cold spring currents in the hours, and even days, before the heavy hatch begins. DAVE HUGHES

The author high-sticking a couple of Pheasant Tail nymphs on the swing with a long rod, early in the BWO hatch on the Bighorn River in Montana. JIM SCHOLLMEYER

hook quickly, even with that long rod that softened any set. Instead, it was best to simply hold on, let the trout hook themselves, not respond at all until they were on and knew it and were angry at that sting, running away from it. The best way to make it all work was exactly the way Davy Wotton taught me on the White River: Loft the rod tip high, let the line drop in a constant curve from the rod top to the water, watch that curve, and set the hook only when the line began to rise higher in the air, indicating a take, or the point where it entered the water hesitated, even moving off a bit upstream or straight away. Then a trout was on and setting the hook would cause it to dance.

This method—swinging nymphs and even wet flies that represented the hatches that were trickling off—worked well for about three days. Then the weather warmed, the BWO hatch started to come off in more normal abundance, trout turned their attention to floating duns, and my swung nymph tactic no longer interested them. That's all right. My interest turns away from sunk flies when trout begin rising in sufficient numbers that they can be pinpointed and cast to with dry flies and some hope of success.

That's another and more major spring tactic: fishing dry flies and emergers over rising trout. You know how to do it better than I do, though, so I'm not going to bother you about that. I've just given you some hints about what to do when what you'd really like to do isn't working very well in the spring conditions of the moment.

# Rods, Flies, and the Rest for Spring

A trout river in spring is an iffy proposition, with exceptions. The standard exception is the spring creek, a stream rising from water that settled deep into the earth over enough years to have forgotten the whims of its seasons—a spring creek emerges from the ground at one volume and one temperature year-round. A tailwater, a river emerging from a dam, is another exception when it's held down to a comfortable level during wet months by some kindly agency or another. Of course there's always the chance of a low-water year on a freestone river, a river neither stalled by dams nor fed by springs but gathering its flow straight off the surface, a year when runoff and rain are light and the river holds its shape from March through May and June—good for spring fishing but a price may be paid in late season when the water is low and warm and the trout are stressed.

A river running high may offer good fishing—provided it's not running *too* high. CAROL ANN MORRIS

Most rivers of modest volume or smaller are freestone rivers, and in a typical year most of them are swollen in spring with rain and melting snow. That's why I mentioned that iffy proposition—your favorite stream may be running a good temperature for trout in early April and may even be sprinkled with hatching caddisflies or mayflies or both or more, but it may also be brown and up churning through bankside trees and brush. If the water's that high, you probably ought to find a spring creek or a tailwater river in good shape, or try lake fishing, and leave your favorite stream and its trout to settle down.

But your favorite trout stream may be fishable in spring. High water is OK so long as it's not extreme. I've caught a lot of trout in water still tinted from near-flooding and still tugging at the brush that lines its banks. Trout have to eat, high water or not. And if they're eating you have a shot at them.

## Clothing

March and April are particularly uncertain months for weather in much of North America, so a good place to start with springtime fishing on trout rivers is

and you could catch a cold or even turn hypothermic. Waders are wise even if you plan not to wade (some rivers really don't require wading). Waders keep you dry in a downpour and provide constant considerable warmth. A hat for UV protection and warmth, finger-less gloves to keep the chill off the hands, heavy socks (and a spare pair in case your waders leak), and you're set.

## Wading—Go with Caution, and a Friend

A fishing partner makes particular sense when you'll spend the day wading a high, angry river—having someone to occasionally check on you is good insurance.

You probably already know how to wade, so I'll just say, wade with caution. Don't push your limits and back off whenever your instincts tell you to—this is not that same gentle river you cross with ease in August. High rivers run quick and strong. And if you ever use a wading staff (I always do), use one on rivers running high.

## Rods and Lines

I've always had a soft spot for 6-weight lines and rods. No matter what I need to do on a trout river—drop a size 20 midge emerger upstream of the nose of a trout picking at the water's surface or heave a big weighted nymph and an indicator along with some split shot way out there—a 6-weight setup seems to help me do it. And if the river's of good size, I want that rod to carry some power. (Remember: Many rivers that run light in summer and require only comfortable casts may run heavy in spring and demand long casts from awkward places. I fished an Idaho creek last May I couldn't have waded across if a free bamboo rod waited on the other side, then returned to it in August to cross it without going over my calves or slowing the tempo of my gait. Fishing was good both times, by the way, but very different.)

Some fly fishers feel a 6-weight line is too heavy, even unsporting, on a trout stream, and they have every right to their opinions. Some even think a 5-weight line is too much. Fine. I just want to be there to see them toss the kind of weight a high river requires for springtime nymph fishing on a feathery

clothing and waders. Layers of clothing are always a good idea when fishing and make especially good sense in spring, when an icy morning may build to shirtsleeve temperatures by afternoon. One or even two fairly light shirts under a heavier one and per-haps a coat over it all provide a lot of range. If a day warms, just run back and drop off a shirt or two in the car or stuff what you take off into a small pack or the back of your fishing vest. Pants can be layered too, perhaps a pair of sweatpants or fleece pants over or under light pants of quick-drying material.

A waterproof jacket is a requirement if there's any chance of rain—a soaking in chilly spring is misery

If trout are rising anywhere on a brimming springtime river, it's probably happening in softer flows off the main current.

**Right:** A 5-weight line and rod are the first choice of many fly fishers for nearly all trout fishing, but I prefer a 6-weight outfit like this one for swollen springtime rivers.

PHOTOS BY CAROL ANN MORRIS

3-weight line. I'm not saying they can't do it, I'm just saying I want to watch. Should be entertaining.

## Flies

On to a subject as dear to my heart as any: flies. Fly patterns for brimming springtime rivers run the gamut—I've seen trout well away from the force of a high April river sipping tiny midges in an eddy and requiring tiny emerger flies on light tippets, but I've many times fished big gaudy nymphs and streamers in such rivers. So it's more useful to look at generalities when it comes to spring flies for rivers than to sift through the endless variations of conditions, water types, hatches, and the rest.

The first thing you need to know about fly selection for trout rivers in spring is that the pressure's off. With the trout having just faced a winter of distractions—mainly survival, with feed scarce and the dangers of flooding and ice coming in steady waves—those fish are as close to gullible as you're likely to ever find them (with the exception of spawning, a time when trout are reckless and weak and should be left to their business). So, hungry and retaining only a dim memory of their usual caution, the trout may not much care what fly you give them, and in a high flow they may not much care *how* you give it to them. Easy trout can be refreshing if you're used to walking that tightrope of selecting just the right fly of just the right size and delivering it with stealth and gentle accuracy. So loosen up. Tie on some big weird dry fly, maybe one of those crazy variations of the Chernobyl Ant or a gaudy nymph—it might be deadly.

If you plan to nymph-fish a high river—which is a promising approach—a trailer rig is a good way to start. A trailer rig includes two nymphs, one tied on a foot or so of tippet coming off the bend of the other nymph's hook. Typically the top nymph in the rig is big and heavy, made with plenty of thick lead wire (better yet, lead-substitute wire) at its core, and maybe a big metal bead for a head. Because such big stoneflies as the Golden Stonefly of the West and the Giant Black Stonefly of the East are normally down there as nymphs nearly full-grown for their late-spring and summer hatching, a stonefly nymph imitation is a good choice for the big nymph in your rig. Perhaps a Bitch Creek or Kaufmann Stone.

For the trailer nymph I tend to think of an attractor such as my Gabriel's Trumpet or an imitation of a mayfly nymph such as the old reliable Gold-Ribbed Hare's Ear, which a trout might take as an immature stonefly, either one in size 12 or 14.

But the trailer nymph can be as big and heavy as the fly higher up the rig, and because of the extra weight another big nymph can add, perhaps it should be. So you might have a convincing Beadhead Morristone as one nymph and a silly Beadhead Yuk Bug as the other. Why not?

**Below:** Trout are probably as open-minded as they'll ever be in spring—why not show them something odd and flashy, such as an attractor nymph or egg fly? Perhaps an imitative or flashy attractor streamer?

CAROL ANN MORRIS

# Skip Morris

Streamers in spring? Absolutely. Expect to work them near the banks on sinking-tip lines. A small trout or sculpin imitation such as a Woolhead Sculpin should do it. If other little fishes are present in your rivers, imitations of them make perfect sense. But remember: The trout may be more open-minded than you'll find them later in the season. So why not a silly attractor streamer, maybe a Spruce fly, with a bead, some Flashabou in the body, even a wire rib for a little more shine and to increase toughness? You won't find such a fly in a fly shop or catalog, so you'll have to tie it. If you don't tie, you probably *will* find the old standard Spruce, and it remains a killer.

Dry flies? If the water retains some clarity and there are places where a trout can take something off the surface without struggling against a torrent, you bet. It may surprise you, in fact, just how high and angry a river can be and still offer dry-fly fishing. I remember a high-water day on a float trip down Montana's Bitterroot River a few years ago when we threw large drys from morning until we hit the boat landing in late afternoon. After a blast of heavy rain during our last hour of the drift, the river seemed to rise visibly before us as our friend headed upstream to pick up his truck and trailer. I waded out along the edge of the flow and started tossing a gaudy Chernobyl Ant variation around the flooded brush that acted like a baffle against the current. I had time to move only one fish, but it was a dandy: around 16 inches of deep, healthy cutthroat trout, a great splash of crimson along each cheek and flank. The handsomest trout of the day. It seemed to rise with perfect contentment not over riverbed but over grassy flooded bank.

High water doesn't preclude insect hatches. If some eddy or soft current off the rushing main flow is speckled with hatching Western March Brown mayflies (and I've seen it), fine; show those trout rising to them a tan-bodied Thorax Dun or Brooks's Sprout.

As I said, trout-river fishing varies in spring. It can be like summer fishing with the river in fine condition and warm sunshine on your back. Or it can be cruel, the river churning with color and the fishing a struggle. But if spring fishing can be done, it's probably worth doing, especially after winter's long stretch of limited fishing opportunities.

SKIP MORRIS

## BEADHEAD MORRISTONE, GOLDEN STONE

*Skip Morris*

| | |
|---|---|
| **Hook:** | #6-10 standard to heavy wire, 2X, 3X, or 4X long (slow curve optional) |
| **Bead:** | Brown, copper, black, or gold, metal |
| **Thread:** | Brown 6/0 or 3/0 |
| **Weight:** | Lead-substitute wire |
| **Tail:** | A V cut from the tip of a mottled brown hen-saddle (hen back) hackle |
| **Rib:** | Medium-thick copper wire |
| **Body:** | Brown fuzzy Antron, wool yarn, or chenille |
| **Wing Case:** | Two sections of pheasant-tail fibers, one bound atop the other, light side down |
| **Legs:** | The body of the hen-saddle hackle used for the tail |

**Notes:** As an imitation of the Golden Stone nymph, the Morristone Golden version has never failed me. The soft tail and legs move freely and convincingly in current. You can find tying instructions for tying the Morristone in both *Fly Tying Made Clear and Simple* and *Trout Flies for Rivers*. I like to wind a layer of thick wire over the center two-thirds of the shank, bind that wire, and then wind a short length of thinner wire over the thorax area and bind it. The trick to winding both the yarn and rib up the shank and behind and in front of the pheasant fibers and leg hackle is to draw the pheasant and hackle forward and bind them loosely at the hook's eye, wind the yarn up to the pheasant and hackle, and then unwind the thread turns holding them. Do the same for the rib.

**THORAX DUN,
WESTERN MARCH BROWN**

**JAZZED UP, BEAD-HEAD SPRUCE FLY**

SKIP MORRIS

SKIP MORRIS

| | |
|---|---|
| **Hook:** | #10-16 light wire, standard length or 1X long |
| **Thread:** | Tan 8/0 |
| **Tail:** | Dark ginger hackle fibers, split |
| **Abdomen:** | Tan buoyant dubbing |
| **Wing:** | Mallard-dyed wood duck, one wing |
| **Hackle:** | Dark ginger, one, spiraled over the front half of the shank and trimmed underneath |
| **Thorax:** | The same dubbing used for the abdomen |

**Notes:** This Thorax Dun—the one that's been popular for the past couple of decades at least—is actually very different from Vince Marinaro's original. But it became popular for the obvious reasons.

| | |
|---|---|
| **Hook:** | #4-12 standard to heavy wire, 2X or 3X long |
| **Bead:** | Gold metal |
| **Thread:** | Black or red 8/0, 6/0, or 3/0 |
| **Tail:** | Peacock sword |
| **Rib:** | Gold or amber copper wire |
| **Body:** | Red Flashabou or Krystal Flash for the rear half and peacock herl for the front half |
| **Wing:** | Two badger hen-neck or large rooster-saddle hackles curving away from each other |
| **Hackle:** | Badger, the same kind of hackle used for the wings |

*Skip Morris*

Many different nymphs and larvae call rocky runs like this home, as do many trout. One important insect that often goes unnoticed is the little Saddle-Case caddis. DAVE HUGHES

*Rick Hafele*

# Glossosoma
## The Little Caddis That Can

One of my favorite spring hatches is a small caddis. It occurs throughout North America but flies under the backcast of most anglers. This is the Saddle-Case caddis, a little caddis that belongs to the family Glossosomatidae. Though small in size, this family is large with six different genera and about eighty species in North America.

*Glossosoma* like cobble and small boulders in moderate to fast water, which accounts for one of their common names, the mountain caddis. RICK HAFELE

Two genera, *Agapetus* and *Glossosoma*, account for over half the total species in the family, and while *Glossosoma* species produce the most important hatches for anglers across the continent, species of *Agapetus* are as widespread, only much smaller and therefore more likely to go unnoticed.

With over fifty species spread across all regions of the country, it shouldn't be a surprise that these little guys get called a lot of different names by fly fishers, including Saddle-Case caddis, Igloo-Case caddis, Tiny Black Short-Horned sedge, Little Brown Short-Horned sedge and Little Tan Short-Horned sedge. Excellent photos of all the different stages of the major genera can be found in Thomas Ames Jr.'s impressive book, *Caddisflies: A Guide to Eastern Species for Anglers and Naturalists*.

Given the large number of species, these little caddis express a range of colors and sizes, and even entomologists are challenged to distinguish specific species. The angler is best served by learning to recognize the family and then adjusting pattern size and color as needed. To that end here are some key features shared by all members of Glossosomatidae.

## LARVA

- Case made of small gravel creating a domelike or igloolike shape that completely covers the larva so that no head or legs are exposed. Cases range from $1/8$ to $3/8$ inch across.
- The underside of the case includes a short strap or "saddle" of silk across the middle of the larva. This strap helps anchor the larva inside the case, and gives the family one of its principle common names, Saddle-Case caddis.
- Inside the case, larvae tend to be pale dirty yellow to almost white in color. The head and first thoracic segment are dark brown to black.
- Anal prolegs are short and partially attached to the abdomen.
- Overall length of mature larvae ranges from $1/8$ to $1/4$ inch and imitated with patterns sized 16 to 22. (Some less common species are much smaller.)

## PUPA

- Develop under domed case sealed inside a thin silk cocoon.
- Size and color similar to mature larva.
- Head, thorax, and wing cases light brown to black.
- Well-developed hind legs used for swimming.

## ADULT

- 1/8 to 1/4 inch long (size 16 to 22).
- Wings dark charcoal gray to dirty gray, sometimes with light spots.
- Body dark brown to dark gray.
- Antennae shorter than body, thus one of their common names—the short-horned sedge.

These caddis are referred to as the "mountain caddisflies" by Herbert Ross, one of the world's foremost authorities on caddisflies, due to their preferred habitat: small to medium-size mountain streams. They are not restricted to smaller streams, however, as many large rivers also have excellent populations. They do prefer cooler streams and generally occur in medium to fast water reaches. A few species have adapted to warm waters. Because they prefer cool mountain streams, the majority of species occur in the Rocky Mountains from Canada south to the Southwestern states and west to the Pacific Coast. Only a few species live in Midwestern and Eastern streams, but the species that do occur there can be

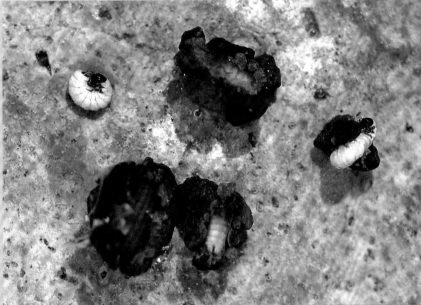

**Left:** Saddle-Case caddis larvae live under small dome-shaped cases. While hidden most of the time, they can drift in large numbers during molts. DAVE HUGHES **Below:** Saddle-Case caddis pupa showing the typical pale color. The dark wing pads indicate this pupa is mature and close to emerging. RICK HAFELE

**Left:** The small adults are most often seen running around on shoreline grasses. RICK HAFELE

quite abundant and just as important as their more diverse Western cousins.

Larvae feed by scraping diatoms off the exposed surfaces of submerged stones. They move about protected under their domed cases leaving small bare feeding tracks across the rocks showing where they have removed the thin layer of diatoms and algae. As they grow, larvae molt five times, and with each molt they must replace their case with a new, larger one. For most caddis larvae this is not a hazardous process, as they make their small case larger by adding on to it. But Saddle-Case caddis must start from scratch each time they need a larger case. As a result the larvae are exposed and unprotected for a time and many end up drifting in the current. Gary LaFontaine, in his book *Caddisflies*, suggests the molts and resulting drift behavior often happen en masse, creating significant feeding by trout on the little larvae. I have no idea how to determine when such drift activity occurs short of putting a net in the current to collect them, a level of effort that's impractical for most fishing situations.

The bottom line is this: Saddle-Case caddis larvae can be important to imitate when drifting in large numbers, so carry some small nymph patterns to match them. LaFontaine recommends that where Saddle-Case caddis are abundant, the larval drift is common and important enough that small imitative nymph patterns are effective searching flies worth trying whenever you are nymph fishing.

Mature larvae begin pupation by first tightly securing their cases to rock surfaces with silk thread. Then inside the case they spin a brown silk cocoon within which they molt into pupae. Here the pupae remain hidden for up to four weeks while they develop. Larvae often congregate together on specific stones before latching down their cases to pupate, so it is not uncommon to pick up a bowling-ball-size rock from a riffle and find dozens of little cases clustered together. When I find such clusters I often pull off two

or three and open them to see their size and color and how mature the pupae are inside. A typical fully developed pupa runs a size 16 to 20 with a pale yellowish pink to very light tan abdomen, a tan thorax and head, and brownish black wing pads. When I find mature pupae, my heart rate immediately jumps and I check my caddis fly box to make sure I have some little pupa patterns to match, for when an emergence occurs trout can't resist them and I know I'll be in for some great fishing.

Saddle-Case caddis pupae are vigorous swimmers. When they leave their protective cases on the bottom of medium to fast riffles, they kick their way to the surface using their hind legs, creating a rapid, jerky swimming action. Sometimes the pupae swim toward rocky shorelines, where they crawl out just above the waterline to emerge into adults. Once while standing in a riffle fishing, my legs apparently looked like a suitable rock, for when I looked down dozens of little pupae were crawling up my waders to hatch. Other times pupae simply swim up to the surface and adults emerge in the surface film. In either case the swimming pupae are prime targets for feeding fish.

The exact timing of emergence activity is difficult to predict and can occur any time from midmorning

**Below:** A cluster of Saddle-Case caddis larvae ready to pupate sit on the side of a small boulder in a quick run. RICK HAFELE

The current seams below this riffle are the perfect place to find *Glossosoma* pupae swimming up to the surface, or later in the day, adults diving below the surface to lay their eggs. RICK HAFELE

to late afternoon—say 9:00 or 10:00 a.m. to 5:00 or 6:00 p.m.—depending on the weather, water temp, time of year, and specific species emerging. Whenever you notice clustered cases on the rocks, watch the water carefully throughout the day for hatch activity.

Once emerged, the adults also produce some great fishing. Adults are similar in size to their pupae—size 16 to 20 with some species much smaller. Their dark brown to charcoal gray wings may or may not be flecked with light gold markings. Their small size and the fast water from which they emerge make them hard to see on the water. I see adults most often running quickly, and seemingly randomly, over grass stems and branches of shrubs along the bank.

Fish take adults when they first pop out on the surface. Adults at times run across the surface toward shore rather than take off from the surface quickly. This can entice trout to no end. Then, after spending a few days on shore mating, the females return to the water to lay eggs. For this they don't just drop to the

surface but actually dive below the surface and swim to the bottom to lay eggs. Again this generally occurs in choppy water, so you will be unlikely to see clearly what's going on. In general if you see lots of adults around shore, then be prepared to match them with drys on the surface or with diving adult patterns below it. Here's how Thomas Ames Jr. describes the situation during egg laying in his book *Caddisflies*:

There is clearly some trial and error involved in deciding how to present a fly when short-horned sedges are laying their eggs. Some fish will take them as they come to rest on the surface. Others wait until the fly sinks underneath. Still others want a moving fly.

Ames's description captures the challenges of presentation for this little caddis. When fishing adults I typically start with a dry fly on the surface. I dead-drift it the first half of the cast and then let it swing

A pair of mating *Glossosoma* adults are dwarfed by a Salmonfly. On more than one occasion I've had trout ignore the large Salmonfly but readily take a little caddis dry. Why? I have no idea! RICK HAFELE

with some action the last half. If that fails I put on a small split shot and sink the fly below the surface. I might also change flies to a diving adult pattern. Cast up and across so the fly has time to sink and then let it swing up toward the surface as it drifts downstream. Watch the surface for signs of rising fish and any clues as to where or how they may be feeding. Egg-laying activity generally occurs in the late afternoon to early evening.

This little caddis isn't important just during late winter/early spring. Because most streams, especially Western streams, have multiple species in them, hatches start as early as mid-February and continue well into June. Another flurry of activity typically occurs in the fall starting in September and continuing until mid-November.

This is one caddis you will have plenty of chances to match, and you'll have lots of fun once you figure it out. Unfortunately, for a variety of reasons, many anglers completely miss this hatch. First, the larvae only show themselves as a little dome of small gravel stuck to a rock. If you don't recognize this for what it is, you won't suspect it's anything important. Second,

pupae are very small. A size 16 is a monster, and most will be 18s or 20s and even smaller. So again unless you look closely and know what to look for, you won't notice them. Third, the hatch occurs in riffles where the pupae and adults are even harder to see on the surface.

Many anglers aren't aware how important these little caddis can be. To determine their importance in your streams look for two clues. One, the clustered cases of larvae or pupae on cobble-size rocks in riffles. Look for them by simply picking up a few rocks from a riffle. When you find them, pull off some cases to determine if there are mature pupae inside. Second, look for the little dark gray adults running around on shoreline grasses and shrubs. When you find a lot of adults, remember that sometime during the day pupae are swimming to the surface and females are returning to lay eggs. If you can't see feeding fish, put on a pupa pattern and fish it close to the bottom with a nymph rig through choppy riffles. If you do see fish feeding, fish the pupa pattern near the surface or use an adult pattern on or beneath the surface.

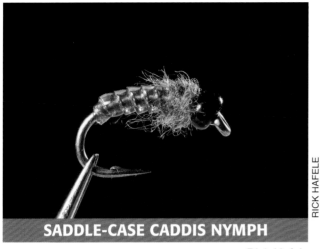

**SADDLE-CASE CADDIS NYMPH**

*Rick Hafele*

| | |
|---|---|
| **Hook:** | #16-18, 1X short scud hook |
| **Thread:** | Tan 8/0 |
| **Head:** | Black bead |
| **Body:** | Medium V-rib, shrimp color |
| **Thorax and Legs:** | Light to dark brown dubbing |

**DIVING CADDIS**

*Rick Hafele*

| | |
|---|---|
| **Hook:** | #16-20 dry-fly hook |
| **Thread:** | Brown 8/0 |
| **Body:** | Dark brown dubbing |
| **Wing:** | White Z-Lon |

**SADDLE-CASE CADDIS PUPA**

*Rick Hafele*

| | |
|---|---|
| **Hook:** | #16-18, 1X short scud hook |
| **Thread:** | Tan 8/0 |
| **Head:** | Black bead |
| **Rib:** | Fine gold wire |
| **Body:** | Dirty white to pale yellow dubbing |
| **Thorax and Legs:** | Dark gray CDC fibers |

**ADULT SADDLE-CASE CADDIS**

*Rick Hafele*

| | |
|---|---|
| **Hook:** | #16-20 dry-fly hook |
| **Thread:** | Brown 8/0 |
| **Body:** | Medium to dark brown dubbing |
| **Wing:** | Dark gray CDC tips tied over back |

Rick Hafele fishing a dry fly up the sort of grassy bank on the Owyhee River where female *Skwala* often launch themselves for the long surface swim that either ends in depositing their eggs into the water or getting themselves deposited into the jaws of a big brown trout. DAVE HUGHES

# Hooked on *Skwala*

*Skwala* stoneflies are among those rare aquatic insects so little known, or its importance so recently noticed, that it goes by its Latin genus name rather than a raft of confusing common names . . . though perhaps in some regions the term Brown Willow fly applies to it rather than to the more likely suspect, a variation of the slightly larger and much more common Golden Stone. Two species of this early season stonefly, *Skwala curvata* and *S. americana*, are distributed in waters from the Rockies to the Pacific Coast. They are so similar that you'll find no need to tell them apart, fortunately, because I'd be unable to do it myself.

# Dave Hughes

They're also hard to distinguish, in the nymph stage, from the much more widespread Golden Stoneflies. They're just a bit smaller when mature, size 8 and 10 on long-shank hooks, rather than size 6, and also more slender. Perhaps this similarity is beneficial to the angler. The same fly patterns that you fish for the larger nymphs, downsized a bit, will work as well for the smaller *Skwala*. That is not true for the more important adult stage.

*Skwala* populations are distributed broadly throughout the West, but they're more often sparse than abundant. They're also somewhat cryptic in the adult stage, hiding deep in streamside grasses rather than clambering about like the bigger, and therefore more visible, Golden Stones that hatch later in spring. *Skwala* seldom arrive on the water in bunches, in my own experience, and are at times so sparse that they could be called scant. But they hatch early in the season, when trout are hungry, and they are large insects compared to the more common fare at that time of year—the midges and glossosomid caddis that Rick and Skip are covering as more important to them, and of course, the Blue-Winged Olive mayflies that are so important to all of us in the first months of the year.

My admonition here is to watch carefully for *Skwala* adults, even if they're only occasional. If they're around at all, trout will be aware of it, and they'll know what to do about it. You should, too. The trout that work on them are very often large.

*Skwala* nymphs are elongated, slender, and have little taper from front to back. They have two antennae, two tails, and vermiculated patterning on their heads and thoracic segments. All of these things could be said about Golden Stone nymphs as well. You'll often collect them in the same sort of water, usually riffles or rocky runs. If you're intent on separating one from another, then turn the insect over; the *Skwala*

lacks the dominant bushy gills that you'll find on the thorax of the Golden Stone, looking almost like white armpit hair. Trout fail to notice the lack of armpit hair when they whack an imitation, which is why you can use the same fly for *Skwala* as you do for Golden Stone nymphs.

*Skwala* are distributed in all sorts of Western waters, but I've found them most common in small to medium-size tailwaters. That finding is likely related to my preference to fish those kinds of waters in February and March, when dams tame flows and also tend to clarify the water, making conditions more acceptable for fishing than they often are on freestone streams at the same time of year. Most of my own fishing over *Skwala* has been on the Crooked River in Oregon, the Yakima River in Washington, the South Fork of the Boise River in Idaho, and the famous Owyhee River, on the border between Oregon and Idaho. But it would be foolish to overlook the

*Skwala* nymph (*Skwala americana*) on the left and a Golden Stone nymph (*Calineuria californica*) on the right. Both are active predators feeding on any small aquatic insect they can catch. Note the bushy gills at the base of the legs of the Golden Stone. *Skwala* nymphs have no such gills. RICK HAFELE

Dave fishing—and playing a fish—close to shore near the still bare willows of the Owyhee River in Oregon. RICK HAFELE

hatch on Chuck Stranahan's water on the Bitterroot River in Montana, where it might be most famous. You should get your information on that hatch, which is a bit later toward spring than it is farther to the west, from Chuck in his shop in Hamilton, right on the river. Obviously, he'll also have the fly patterns that best match it there.

Nymph patterns need not be specific to the *Skwala*, though you can find lots of folks who disagree with me, and you'll also find that each of them offers an excellent pattern. You can use downsized Golden Stone dressings, or upsized standards such as the Gold-Ribbed Hare's Ear. I caught a bunch of trout on *Skwala* water once fishing a large Copper John while I waited for the scant hatch to start and for the trout to begin tipping their attention upward. I asked a couple of the larger, and supposedly smarter, trout why they had taken the Copper John. They complained about being hungry at that time of year, about the sparsity of other things to eat, and about the slight but sneaky resemblance between the brash nymph and the few natural *Skwala* they'd been able to hunt

down. The truth is that you can fish the soft water near riffles and rocky runs with a Copper John or Beadhead Gold-Ribbed Hare's Ear and do quite well, but you'd also be very wise to drop a size 16 generic nymph off its stern, on about 10 or 12 inches of lighter tippet, in case trout down there take a look at the bigger *Skwala* nymph and decide they don't like it.

Whatever fly you fish for the nymph, and whether you rig it with a point fly or not, be sure to get it to the bottom and fish it dead-drift. The naturals live in fairly fast water, among bottom stones, but they must make the migration to shore before they're able to emerge into adults. Trout line up and wait for them in the softer water inside those riffles and runs. You won't be able to see the trout, so the critical skill you need to develop is recognition of the type of water where the natural insects live, and then the nearest somewhat soft water to the edges of it, where trout can hold along the bottom without fighting a strong and cold current.

Use the indicator-and-split-shot rig, with enough weight to get the nymph, or nymphs, to the bottom,

# Dave Hughes

## An Ethical Dilemma

I've mentioned that *Skwala* are often scant, that you can sometimes find one or two in streamside grasses, and that the best way to locate a trout is to follow the float of an adult *Skwala* on the water and watch for a big nose to poke out to take it. Now I ask you: If you were to find a *Skwala* adult crawling happily around in the grass, would it be ethical to capture it and throw it out onto water where you suspect there might be a big and hungry trout, in order to follow its float and thereby pinpoint the lie of that trout?

We both know what Rick and Skip would do, because they're both scoundrels. We might both have a suspicion about what I'd do, but neither of us is sure. I can't answer what you would do; I'm not even sure what you *should* do! ∎

Hafele with a fat brown that inhaled a *Skwala* dry fly. Proof that fishing is easy when trout are on the hunt for *Skwala*. Hafele commented: "I did not locate this brown through any unscrupulous use of a live adult!" (See the ethical dilemma sidebar.) DAVE HUGHES

and enough indicator to float with all that weight down there. Leave enough scope in the leader between the nymphs and the indicator so that the flies bounce on the bottom rather than dangle a foot or two above it. If there is a second secret beyond reading the water right to find the trout, it's rigging right to get the nymph, or brace of them, down to where the trout will be sure to notice them.

Fish them dead-drift, painting parallel brush-strokes along the bottom with them, in what the great Gary Borger called the "Shotgun Method" in his seminal but still excellent *Nymphing*.

*Skwala adults* are less like Golden Stones than their earlier nymphal stage. They are concolorous, with a single shade of grayish brown on the back and wings, though it's somewhat lighter on the underside. The females have two full sets of wings, in normal stonefly fashion, but the males are more often than not brachypterous: short-winged. Whether winged or not, it's not common to see *Skwala* adults in the air. They prefer to crawl in the grasses and launch them-selves onto the water by crawling rather than flying.

I've seen adult females hike out of streamside grass, sere and brown and dry at that time of year, as if they were early hominids emerging out of forests. I've also seen them tiptoe out on fallen grass stems, as if they were walking planks, and then drop onto the water and begin long floats downstream.

*Skwala* show a couple of different behaviors when on the water. Mostly they just float amiably and peaceably along, letting the current take them where it will. This is almost always on long stretches of fairly calm water. The second behavior seems to be a sudden panicked scramble to walk on the water, either out to where they want to deposit their eggs or back to the safety of the shore from which they so recently departed.

I've already mentioned, to the point where you're about to turn your head aside at the cliché, that *Skwala* are more often scant than abundant. The first thing you need to do when you suspect they're around is search streamside grasses and watch the water carefully for them. They'll appear one at a time; you'll need to notice them when they do. As soon as you spot one on the water, cease casting, get out your handy Nikon binoculars if you must, and follow its drift. Sometimes it will float 10 feet and go down in a swirl. Other times it will float 100 or even 200 feet. But the almost inevitable end of a *Skwala* adult on trout water is a nose lofted out, and a quiet death. I've never seen it announced with any fanfare. If you're not watching, you'll never see it happen. That's why I recommend you do more watching than casting when you're fishing water with trout of good size and you've spotted any *Skwala* adults in the grasses or on the waters.

In my own interviews with trout, they've told me that so early in the season, when fishing over such a large adult insect, exact imitation is less important than getting something the right size over the right spot. That said, it's a fun hatch for which to create your own dressing, and you're almost sure to be rewarded, because trout feeding on *Skwala* are almost sure to take it.

I've had success with Jim Schollmeyer's Foam Skwala dressing, with an Egg-Laying Skwala with a hair wing, and also with a Deer Hair Caddis tied in a large enough size to imitate the natural.

Presentation should be a combination of dead-drift float with occasional hops and skitters and skates inserted to imitate both the free float and panicked skating of the naturals. If you're covering a sighted rise and the first couple of drifts fail to move the trout, add a skitter to your next presentation to wake the trout up, let it know another meal is floating over its head. Most often, because the females launch themselves from shore and float parallel to it, trout will feed within 5 to 10 feet of the bank, and you should focus your fishing there. But follow the drift of any natural you spot on the water. When a nose pokes out to take it, reel up, and move immediately into position to fish over that trout. Don't take your time to fish your way upstream or down to it; it might have moved by the time you get there. If a trout marks itself, move to it instantly, and catch it as quickly as you can.

**Below:** A warm afternoon in late winter is a beautiful time to be on the water, and a great time for *Skwala* adults to be running around. Don't look for them in the air. Adults rarely fly, so look for them along the bank in the willows and grass. DAVE HUGHES

# Dave Hughes

That is what *Skwala* fishing means to me, more than any other early fishing: spotting a natural on the water, following its drift, watching for a nose to poke out, moving instantly into position to take a shot at it. I'll confess it's a bit like hunting, though I personally don't like to confuse fishing with hunting . . . but the analogy can be allowed to continue: Trout that feed on early *Skwala* are often such a size that they can be considered big game.

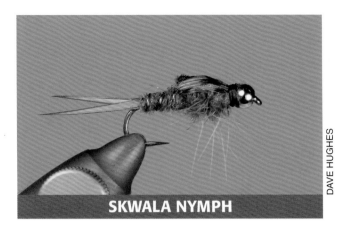

## SKWALA NYMPH

DAVE HUGHES

| | |
|---|---|
| **Hook:** | #10-12, 3X long |
| **Head:** | Gold bead |
| **Weight:** | Ten to fifteen turns non-lead wire |
| **Thread:** | Brown 3/0 or 6/0 |
| **Tails:** | Ginger biots, forked |
| **Rib:** | Copper wire |
| **Body:** | Brown-amber dubbing |
| **Wing Case:** | Mottled turkey feather section |
| **Thorax:** | Brown-amber dubbing |
| **Legs:** | Ginger hen hackle fibers |

**Top:** A female *Skwala* drifting on the water and enticing trout. **Right:** Female *Skwala* adult hanging out on some dry shoreline grass stems. Note the small *Glossosoma* caddis adult sharing the stem. **Left:** Male *Skwala* adult. See the short non-functional wings? This is not a genetic malfunction, and is typical of *Skwala* males. Females can fly, but rarely do so. The result: Fish dry flies close to the banks. PHOTOS BY RICK HAFELE

## BEADHEAD GOLD-RIBBED HARE'S EAR

DAVE HUGHES

| | |
|---|---|
| **Hook:** | #8-12 standard nymph |
| **Bead:** | Gold |
| **Weight:** | Twelve to fifteen turns non-lead wire |
| **Thread:** | Brown 6/0 |
| **Tail:** | Hare's mask guard hairs |
| **Rib:** | Gold oval tinsel |
| **Body:** | Hare's mask fur |
| **Wing Case:** | Dark turkey feather section |
| **Thorax:** | Hare's mask fur, with guard hairs |

# Dave Hughes

**COPPER JOHN**

*John Barr*

| | |
|---|---|
| **Hook:** | #10-12 standard nymph |
| **Bead:** | Gold |
| **Weight:** | Thirteen turns non-lead wire |
| **Thread:** | Black 6/0 |
| **Tails:** | Brown biots, forked |
| **Body:** | Copper wire |
| **Wing Case:** | Black Thin Skin, epoxied |
| **Thorax:** | Peacock herl |
| **Legs:** | Brown hen back fibers |

**SKWALA EGG-LAYER**

| | |
|---|---|
| **Hook:** | #10-12, 2X or 3X long dry fly |
| **Thread:** | Brown 3/0 or 6/0 |
| **Egg Sac:** | Black foam |
| **Tails:** | Ginger biots, forked |
| **Rib:** | Working thread |
| **Body:** | Golden-amber dubbing |
| **Wing:** | Brown bucktail |
| **Hackle:** | Grizzly and ginger mixed, clipped in V-notch |

**FOAM SKWALA**

*Jim Schollmeyer*

| | |
|---|---|
| **Hook:** | #10-12 short shank dry fly |
| **Thread:** | Tan 6/0 |
| **Abdomen:** | Tan Larva Lace foam, extended |
| **Wing:** | Natural tan yearling elk hair |
| **Head:** | Tan Larva Lace foam, bullet style |

**DEER HAIR CADDIS**

*Jim Schollmeyer*

| | |
|---|---|
| **Hook:** | #8-10 standard dry fly |
| **Thread:** | Olive 6/0 |
| **Hackle:** | Dark blue dun, palmered over body |
| **Body:** | BWO Super Fine dubbing |
| **Wing:** | Gray dyed yearling elk hair |

# My Life as a Mayfly

A Pale Morning Dun Speaks:

It's cold on the bottom of a trout stream. Of course, as a coldblooded mayfly nymph adapted to cold-water trout streams, I find it rather comfortable. I'm sitting, along with a half dozen other nymphs, on the bottom of a gentle riffle among golf-ball-to baseball-size stones lazily grazing on diatoms and bits of algae like we've done every day for almost a year now. I find it hard to keep track of time since every day is much like the one before, except that every day there seems to be a few less of us grazing. I've also noticed lately that most of my brothers and sisters around me now have odd growths on their backs shaped like two dark brownish black slippers. I can't see my own back, but it feels different and my skin seems to be getting tighter.

# Rick Hafele

Suddenly a call goes out that an important meeting is scheduled and all the nymphs in my neighborhood must attend. Apparently the chief nymph has something critical to tell us. My buddies and I on the rock can hardly eat as this is the first time such a meeting has ever been called, and we have no idea what could be so important.

Hundreds, hell thousands, of nymphs start moving toward a hollowed-out area surrounded by waving aquatic plants. The afternoon sun reflects off the water, and the sky looks like spilled paint in the water's mirrorlike surface. Crawling along the bottom may look safe, but moving from the rock crevices to the meeting location is risky. If you lose your footing, the current quickly takes you away, and we've been told from our first days as nymphs to stay out of the current at all costs—when you drift away you never come back.

Once gathered together around the aquatic plants, we all settle into a comfortable resting place. Some hang on the leaves of the plants. Others sit in the sand at the base of the stems. I find a nice flat stone off to one side to crawl onto just as the chief nymph stands up on a piece of dead wood lodged in the bottom and begins explaining what is happening.

"Dear brothers and sisters, this is the day you've all been eating for," he begins. "Within the next few days you will change in ways you can't imagine. You've all seen the dark slipperlike growths on everyone's back. And you've felt the tightness of your skin. In the past such feelings meant you needed to find a safe place to hide while your tight outer skin fell off and a new, looser skin took its place. That was then, this is now."

The head nymph pauses, waiting to make sure we are all paying close attention, and then goes on: "The

PHOTOS BY RICK HAFELE

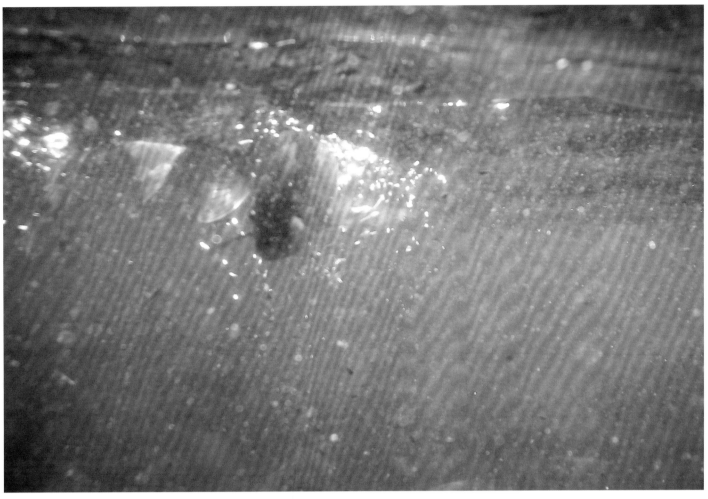

RICK HAFELE

next time you feel the gentle warming of the water, when the late morning sun slowly raises the water temperature, you will have an uncontrollable urge to let go of the bottom and swim toward the surface."

"Yeah, right," I say to the nymph on my left. "That's the last thing I'm going to do. See those fish just above eyeing us? It would be suicide to leave the stream bottom."

The head nymph keeps talking: "You will try to resist, but resistance is futile and only prolongs the inevitable. It is the destiny of every nymph here and across the entire waterway to let go of the bottom and swim for the heavens above."

He now stands straight up on his two back legs using his tails for balance: "I repeat, every nymph here and across the entire waterway will let go of the stream bottom and head for the surface. Many of you won't make it. Some will be eaten just as you leave the cover of the bottom. Others will get swept up in swift currents and carried downstream to waiting

trout. Many of you, however, will make it, and for those, the most amazing thing will happen," he yells at the top of his gills. "Just before you reach the surface you will slip out of your tight skins, and instead of a new nymph skin underneath, you will find you have two pair of wings unfolding from your backs. You will also notice that you are as mute as a clam, as you now have no mouth with which to talk, eat, or even drink a drop of water."

"Whoa, this is getting a little far out," I say as I look over at my buddy on the rock next to me. He looks back and quickly adds, "Why in the world would we all do something so dumb? I'm not going."

The old nymph continues, "Why would you do such a dangerous thing? Well, you may have heard stories that someday you will be able to fly through the air like birds. Of course you didn't believe these fairy tales, but I'm here to tell you now that they are true. If you get to the surface and poke your body through the tough film, you will take off into the air

like snowflakes rising up to the clouds." The old nymph's gills twitch up and down. "Then fly quickly to the nearest tree to hide and wait, for within another 24 hours you will molt your skin one last time."

His large eyes sparkle now as he prepares to finish his speech. "Once you've lost your last skin you will take to the air one more time for a great orgy in the sky. Wild sex for all, after which the ladies will lay their burden of eggs back onto the water's surface. Then all will sleep."

With that the old nymph drops down onto all six legs, walks slowly down the log, and disappears.

"That's the craziest thing I've ever heard," my buddy says, while flicking his tails up and down.

But just then he lets go of the stone he's on, and with a shocked look on his face he begins swimming up. When I look around dozens more, then hundreds more, then thousands more nymphs start swimming up. That's when I feel my own legs let go of the smooth round stone on the bottom and I'm floating downstream in the current.

"Holy crap!" I yell as a nymph next to me disappears into a trout's mouth.

Other trout are swimming by with mouths open, darting left and right. Nymphs are disappearing left

Many PMDs hit the surface looking something like this. Because wings still have to straighten and dry, duns float a long time before flying off the water—a fact trout don't ignore. PHOTOS BY RICK HAFELE

and right as well. I decide it is swim or get eaten, so swim I do. I swim like there's no tomorrow, and then suddenly my skin begins to split open. I'm still a foot or so below the surface.

"Just like the old nymph predicted," I yell, when suddenly I'm unable to speak.

Short crumpled wings poke out of my back, and I notice my body is no longer brown, but a beautiful pale yellow color. It is either by luck or grace that I make it to the surface and then through the surface. Others are there too, but not for long. It's crazy. From above swallows dart down grabbing my kin off the water. From below trout keep coming up, sucking my buddies back down. I flail my new wings until they feel stiff and then cross my tarsi, hoping beyond hope to escape the attacks from above and below. I flap hard, and suddenly, like magic, I feel freedom. I'm flying.

Once I'm in the air, swallows keep coming. One barely misses me but gets a similar looking brother right beside me. As I head for the nearest tree I see a strange creature in the water waving a long slender stem in air. He seems to have one of my kind attached to a thread and is throwing it on the water. It doesn't look much like me I think, but a trout sucks it down and he lets out a yell like some wild creature. I'm not going to complain if there is one less trout eating my buddies.

I land on a leaf and sit perfectly still. I'm so unnerved I don't move a muscle the rest of that day or all that night. Late the next morning I once again have the strangest feeling when suddenly my skin splits open, and within just a minute or two my pale yellow wings are clear as glass and I feel lighter and quite excited.

The late morning air is mild and calm and I can see that many others of my kind also look different than yesterday and have already started to fly off their leaves back into the sky. I think, "Well, no sense in stopping now—let's go for it," and fly off with the others.

We now fill the sky 20 or 30 feet above the water. A swarm of millions, nearly all males, dance up and down in the sunlight. The swallows are back too, but to be honest I don't care. I feel light as goose down as I flap my paper-thin, clear wings and dance up and down several feet through the air. While flitting up and down I strain all thousand facets of my huge

PHOTO BY RICK HAFELE

*Scan to watch Video:*
### PMD Behavior

red eyes to find a pale rusty brown female anywhere in my vicinity. There she is. A few feet above and just ahead of me. I give it all I have and fly in from behind and wrap my long front legs around her thorax. She knows just what to do and in seconds we are dropping slowly toward the water while we hold each other in our one and only embrace.

Just before hitting the water she lets go and flies away. I never see her again. I start twirling in the breeze. I can see a swallow change directions and head my way. The swallow's mouth opens . . .

## More about Pale Morning Duns

Besides having a rather hazardous life with little time to mate and lay eggs, PMDs have a variety of traits that can frustrate fly fishers to no end. For example:

- Who are these guys? PMDs belong to a family of mayflies called Ephemerellidae. This family includes some of the most important mayfly hatches found in North America. In the West, besides PMDs, this family also includes Green Drakes (*Drunella grandis* and *D. doddsi*) and Flavs (*Drunella flavilinea* and *D. coloradensis*). In the East, hatches in this family include the Hendrickson (*Ephemerella subvaria*), Pale Evening Dun (*Ephemerella rotunda* and *E. invaria*), and Sulphur (*Ephemerella dorothea*). The Western PMD belongs to a single species, *Ephemerella excrucians*. If you pay attention to Latin names, however, you may remember that PMDs were once considered two species, *E. inermis* and *E. infrequens*. No longer. Fortunately, trout don't seem to care what Latin name we call them, which is probably a very good thing, since Latin names have a tendency to keep changing.
- PMDs live in a wide range of streams and habitats. For example, you are just as likely to run into a great hatch of PMDs on Silver Creek, a classic spring creek in Idaho, as you are on the Green River, a large tailwater stream in Utah, as you are on a small freestone stream like Rock Creek in Montana. And within each of these stream systems PMD nymphs will be at home in moderate to slow currents where rich beds of aquatic plants grow, and in moderate to fast riffles with small gravel to cobble substrates. Such adaptability means you will find PMDs in most every Western trout stream you fish. A similar level of adaptability occurs within the Eastern/Midwestern species of *Ephemerella*, making them equally important in those regions of the country.
- The emergence behavior of PMDs can be rather confusing and not altogether consistent. Sometimes the nymphs swim all the way up to the surface before the duns wiggle their way out of the nymph's tight exoskeleton. But more often than not the duns escape their nymph's exoskeleton a foot or more below the water's surface so that the dun, with crumpled wings unfolding, rises the rest of the way up and must pierce through the surface film to the surface. This behavior can be critical to recognize if trout are feeding on rising duns below the surface—a common practice. When this occurs a wet fly fished 6 inches to a foot below the surface imitating the submerged duns will generally out-fish dry flies on the surface or little nymph patterns fished just below it.
- Cripples are common. Perhaps due to their emergence behavior, or for some other reason unknown, many of the duns on the surface end up as cripples, meaning instead of sitting upright on the water with straight, erect wings, they lay on their sides with wings dangling in different directions. Dry flies that imitate the nicely formed duns, like a well-tied Compara-dun, can produce well, but often a crumpled, twisted-looking

**Opposite page:** Many types of streams and waters hold good populations of PMDs. PHOTOS BY RICK HAFELE

# Rick Hafele

Examples of typical PMD cripples—duns that didn't quite make it! RICK HAFELE

same time. They are all the same species, *Ephemerella excrucians*. So which color should you use to imitate them? I don't know, and to be honest, I don't think it matters. The common Pheasant Tail Nymph's color seems to fit in the range shown here quite well, and I would say it's as good a choice as any. The same color variation occurs with duns. Once again it leaves me wondering just how important color really is in my fly pattern. Such color differences occur in many other species, not just PMDs, and not just in mayflies. This is also why I find it hard to answer fly tiers when they ask me what color dubbing I use for a particular pattern. They want a specific answer, like "yellow Hare-tron dubbing color number 33." When I say, "Well, something pale yellow to light brown is fine," they don't feel satisfied with my answer. But nature just doesn't fit into neat categories like pale yellow number 33.

- Spinners? As both Dave and Skip discuss in their chapters, PMD spinnerfalls can be a hit-or-miss affair, with misses more common than hits. The problem from my experience is that their spinnerfalls are basically unpredictable. Most of the time you can expect them to occur mid- to late morning or into the early afternoon. But this will vary with weather conditions. Hotter weather will push them earlier in the day and cooler weather later in the day. And some days they just don't seem to show up. When they do show up, however, it is wise to be prepared with a simple Rusty Spinner pattern, usually in a size 16. When a good spinnerfall occurs, trout will take up feeding lanes where they can leisurely sip in these dead little morsels of food. If you get everything right, your fly will be included with their lunch. Eastern hatches of related species, such as the Hendrickson, have more predictable and reliable spinnerfalls with most occurring in the evening.

- Fairly long period of emergence. Another nice thing about PMDs, in the West at least, is that the hatch often continues for weeks and weeks on any given stream. In areas with mild climate, like parts of California and the Pacific Northwest, PMD hatches start around mid- to late May and continue into early or mid-July. In Rocky Mountain states, the hatch typically begins in late June and can continue into August or even September. The Eastern relatives of PMDs tend to have spring

pattern that imitates the cripples will work better. A simple pattern for this is a yellow soft-hackle fly fished flush in the surface film rather than below it. Present it drag-free to rising trout that have refused your nice, neat-looking dry fly and see what happens.

- Color! If there is one thing about PMDs that can send fly tiers, and fly fishers, to the psych ward, it's the range of colors they come in. This is true for both nymphs and duns. The nymphs shown below were collected off the same rock at the

Two PMD duns showing common differences in color (male above and female right). These were collected from different streams, but such color variation is common among duns on the same stream as well.

PHOTOS BY RICK HAFELE

# Rick Hafele

hatches, starting with the Hendrickson from mid-April to end of May, followed by Pale Evening Duns in May and June, and last the Sulphurs in June and July. Unlike Blue-Winged Olives or *Baetis*, PMDs do not have multiple generations per year, so when the hatch is over on a given stream you won't see them again until the following year.

- Be ready! If you know you will be on a trout stream during PMD season, make sure you have a selection of patterns that cover the nymph, emerger, dun, cripple, and spinner. A key to success during a good hatch is observation. Trout get quite selective to one stage or another during a good hatch, and unless you take the time to see what stage they are actually eating you can waste a lot of casts with the wrong fly. Sit down, watch the fish closely, and then put on a fly that fits the stage they are taking. Size is perhaps the most critical part of matching this hatch, so it also helps to collect a few duns, cripples, spinners, etc. to check that your flies aren't too big. Rarely do we tie on flies that are too small. Following are my go-to patterns for PMDs and their relatives. Adjust size and color as needed.

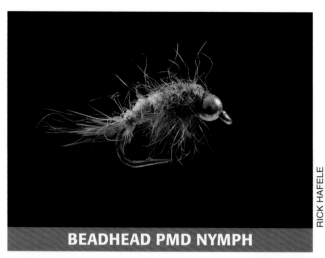

**BEADHEAD PMD NYMPH**

*Rick Hafele*

| | |
|---|---|
| **Hook:** | #14-18 Tiemco 2457 or similar |
| **Head:** | Gold bead |
| **Thread:** | Olive 8/0 |
| **Tail:** | Four to six brown hackle fibers |
| **Rib:** | Copper wire |
| **Body:** | Medium brown to reddish brown dubbing |
| **Thorax:** | Pine squirrel dubbing with guard hairs |

**Wing Case (optional):** Dark turkey tail

**HAIRWING PMD DUN**

*René Harrop*

| | |
|---|---|
| **Hook:** | #14-18 dry-fly hook |
| **Thread:** | Olive 8/0 |
| **Tail:** | Four to six brown hackle fibers |
| **Rib:** | Light brown 6/0 thread |
| **Body:** | Pale yellow dubbing |
| **Wing:** | Bleached deer body hair |
| **Hackle:** | Light brown hackle trimmed flat on bottom |

**YELLOW SOFT-HACKLE**

*Rick Hafele*

| | |
|---|---|
| **Hook:** | #14-18 dry-fly hook |
| **Thread:** | Olive 8/0 |
| **Tail:** | Four to six brown hackle fibers |
| **Rib:** | Fine copper wire |
| **Body:** | Light yellow dubbing |
| **Thorax:** | Pink dubbing |
| **Wing:** | Quail body feather or other gray soft-hackle |

**RUSTY SPINNER**

*Rick Hafele*

| | |
|---|---|
| **Hook:** | #14-18 dry-fly hook |
| **Thread:** | Olive 8/0 |
| **Tail:** | Four to six brown hackle fibers, widely divided |
| **Body:** | Reddish brown dubbing |
| **Thorax:** | Light brown dubbing |
| **Wing:** | White poly |

If you get into a hatch of sulphurs in the East, on water such as Pine Creek in Pennsylvania, you can often match the pale yellow mayflies with patterns tied for the Western PMD hatch. And, of course, the opposite is true: Eastern Sulphur patterns will work quite well for PMDs and even pale evening duns if you encounter them out West.

DAVE HUGHES

*Dave Hughes*

# The Portability of PMD Patterns

Naturally I've fished heavy PMD hatches in the same places you have: on the Deschutes, McKenzie, Henry's Fork of the Snake, Big Hole, Bighorn, and lots of other less famous Western waters. It takes a pretty simple set of patterns to match them; you could use Rick's or Skip's or, as I do, a set winnowed from theirs and many other knowledgeable tiers, as I've listed them in my recent book, *Pocketguide to Western Hatches*.

# Dave Hughes

For the nymph, I use either Rick's Deschutes PMD or the more universal Beadhead Fox Squirrel, originated by the great Dave Whitlock. Both of these patterns are excellent when PMD nymphs are active. But they're also effective as searching nymphs, when no PMDs are moving around, or you have no idea what nymphs trout might be seeing most. There are probably a couple of good reasons these flies catch so many trout when trout are not working PMD nymphs. First, lots of those nymphs are out there, in most Western waters, and trout are always seeing at least a few of them. They have no hesitation to take a nymph that looks at least a little like them. Second, the flies are small, size 16, and it's a given that trout are always on the lookout for nymphs in that size range.

If you've never tried a two-nymph combination, with the larger of the two a size 10 or 12 and the smaller a size 16 or 18, then you've never noticed that trout with few exceptions are caught most often on the smaller nymph. If there is a single thing that will improve your nymph fishing—alongside adding another split shot to get deeper—it's to reduce the size flies you use, with at least one being a size 16 or smaller unless trout are selective to something larger, for example during the Salmonfly migration.

As a consequence of these factors—abundance of naturals and size of the imitations—nymphs tied for

Beahead Fox Squirrel and Rick's Deschutes PMD Nymph. DAVE HUGHES

PMD nymph. DAVE HUGHES

PMD Sparkle Dun and PMD Thorax Dun. DAVE HUGHES

PMD female dun. DAVE HUGHES

Typical slightly riffled PMD water on Oregon's famous Deschutes River. If duns are active, match them with dry flies on the surface. If they're not, tumble PMD nymphs along the bottom. MASAKO TANI

PMDs have a greatly enlarged usefulness to you. It's no secret that the Beadhead Fox Squirrel, in size 16, is my favorite searching nymph, the one I tie on first in any situation where I don't know what might work better, or tie on second, as the point fly in almost any standard two-nymph rig. In other words, unless I know something else will work better, I've almost always got a PMD nymph as part of any searching rig.

One of my flies for the duns makes an attempt to imitate the emerger stage at the same time as it does the dun. It's Craig Mathews's PMD Sparkle Dun, and it's my go-to fly during any PMD hatch. The trailing shuck is amber and represents the cast cuticle of the natural nymph still attached to the dun. PMDs have a high rate of failure; trout often focus on emergers and cripples, and it's handy to have something to imitate them. I like the Sparkle Dun because it's essentially the old, famous Compara-dun tied with the shuck instead of split hackle-fiber tails. If trout happen to be feeding on cripples, it works. If they happen instead

to be feeding on perfect duns, they still seem happy to get a chance to whack a Sparkle Dun . . . I should say sip, because the naturals, when stuck to their shuck, are pinned in the surface; trout rarely take them with bold moves.

The Sparkle Dun is tied for smooth water, which is where PMDs hatch most often. But it doesn't always work, especially if the hatch is on wrinkled water, so I carry a second dressing, Mike Lawson and Vince Marinaro's PMD Thorax Dun. This answers in two situations. First, trout sometimes simply get it in their heads that one pattern isn't acceptable to them, and in that case, you'd better have a second dressing to offer them. Second, in those cases where the water is a bit riffled, then the Sparkle Dun might not have sufficient floatation, and you need a pattern with hackle, hence the Thorax. I'll confess I do not do well with traditional Catskill dry-fly ties for the PMDs; they would work well over trout feeding on the naturals in rough water, but it's rare that PMDs emerge in

# Dave Hughes

**Above:** Ginger Quill Spinner. **Right:** Pale Morning Dun female spinner. PHOTOS BY DAVE HUGHES

water that is any more than slightly bouncy. So I prefer the Thorax Dun, with its hackle trimmed in a V shape on the bottom, rather than the fully hackled Catskill tie.

I haven't gotten into PMD spinnerfalls very often. I don't know if they hit the streams in late evening, after I've gotten scared of rattlesnakes and ghosts and headed in for shelter and dinner or if they come back to the water more often in early morning, before I've got my own engine started. I suspect it's a combination of the two: late evening on cool spring days and early morning on warm summer days. Either way, I haven't bumped into them often enough to tie any more than a couple of color variations of a single dressing, not surprisingly the Red and the Ginger Quill Spinners.

Now I'd like to depart a bit from standard PMD wisdom. I carry the duns and the spinner, just as I do the nymph dressings, wherever I might travel in the fly-fishing world, and though I don't use them as searching patterns, as I do the nymphs, I'm often glad I've got them on me even if no PMDs are in the eyes and minds of any trout at the moment. I'm thinking first of a trip Masako and I took to Pennsylvania to gather photos for the recent second edition

of *Reading Trout Water*; I didn't want all the pictures to be Western. So we spent ten days fishing and photographing famous Pennsylvania streams and had a great time doing it.

The last evening of our trip, we were on Pine Creek, staying at the beautiful Cedar Run Lodge, which is right out of Ernest Schwiebert's early writing. We stopped at a fly shop on Pine Creek before fishing to get a few flies for the Sulphurs, which were then hatching. I peered closely at what I was offered as the best dressings; they were size 16 and were not distinguishable from PMD Compara-duns. I bought a few, just in case, and then we hit the stream, the hatch started, and I tied on my normal size 16 PMD Sparkle Dun. There was one bit of wisdom the fly shop offered, something I'd not have considered: The lady clerk fished the Sulphur hatch the evening before and recommended giving the fly an occasional scoot across the surface during its drift. This was applied, and the trout seemed quite satisfied to take flies tied for the Western hatch.

I've encountered hatches of pale yellowish cream mayflies, in size 16 and 18, in many other states, and even countries, from North Carolina through the more familiar East, Midwest, and West, all the way to

When trout rose to Eastern Sulphurs on Pine Creek, in Pennsylvania, Masako Tani did fine with Western PMD patterns. DAVE HUGHES

When Pale Evening Duns emerge on familiar waters such as the Deschutes, your PMD patterns will usually solve the problem.

**Right:** Pale Evening Duns are a common hatch in late afternoon on many Western rivers.

PHOTOS BY DAVE HUGHES

New Zealand and even Japan. They're not the same species, or even genus, for which we tie our imitations. But trout, as has been said, don't speak Latin, don't key their insects to species before eating them or accepting their imitations. As a consequence, PMD dun dressings can solve problems for you in a lot of places where trout have never had the pleasure of sipping a PMD natural.

Even here in the West, PMD patterns can be applied outside their field of expertise, so to speak. I worked my way up the west bank of the Deschutes River one midsummer day, and toward evening began honing my eye for the Spotted Sedges that normally get active over the water that time of year and that time of day. Instead, a hatch of Pale Evening Duns—PEDs—began emerging sporadically on smooth water about 10 to 20 feet from shore. As light waned the hatch got heavier, and not surprisingly, trout responded by lining up and sipping them.

I don't get into PED hatches often enough to habitually carry specific imitations, though I know what to tie if I encounter them. However, I was out on the river, in the midst of a hatch, and had neither time nor inclination to gallop to camp, tie up a few PED dun patterns, trot back and see if there were any trout left to cast them over . . . or any light left to cast them in. So I peered into my fly boxes, found my perpetual PMD imitations, and tied on the largest of them. It was a size 16. The smallest of the PEDs in the emergence were size 14. Those trout seemed unable to parse out one size from another, and I was able to enjoy fishing that was, perhaps, at least as good as I'd have had with specific PED imitations. Certainly I did better than I'd have done by running back to the tent trailer to tie some or driving to the nearest shop to buy some.

So don't limit your thoughts about PMD imitations to PMD situations. Tie flies that will solve the hatch for you and then carry them with you wherever you fish for trout. It doesn't take a lot of these pale Sulphur-colored dressings to solve situations in a lot of places in the world where trout swim.

**Below:** If you don't have Pale Evening Dun imitations, try your PMD dressings. They'll work. DAVE HUGHES

Skip with a PMD-loving cutthroat trout. CAROL ANN MORRIS

*Skip Morris*

# Dry Flies, Emergers, and the Mainstay Mayfly

Whenever little sunshine-colored mayflies appear, standing high on the current, wings erect, I smile at my good fortune. In the West, only one mayfly is both yellow and small—the Pale Morning Dun or PMD—and it really represents the critical line of support for all Western river mayfly fishing during the long regular season—I've seen PMDs hatch as early as May and as late as mid-October and during all that time between. If our steady, reliable hatches of PMDs went away, the intervals between our days of mayfly fishing on most rivers would be, well . . . disheartening. We'd realize just how good we'd had it thanks to the PMD.

PMD mayfly nymphs can live comfortably in an impressive range of currents, from lazy to lively—that covers a lot of water on a lot of rivers. Expect to encounter PMDs throughout the West. CAROL ANN MORRIS

I've found hatching Pale Morning Duns thick on spring creeks, tailwaters, and freestone rivers—basically every kind of trout stream. Expect to run into the dainty insects often from the Rockies west. However, PMDs need moving water, so you won't find them on lakes.

On the whole I fish nymphs often, but not often for PMDs. Sure, long ago I spent a few summers drifting size 18 Troth Pheasant Tail Nymphs, and later Skip Nymphs, Dark, through Oregon's Metolius River knowing full well the rainbows took them to be nymphs of the Pale Morning Dun. And I've done the same in other rivers well-stocked with PMD nymphs. But I'll bet I've fished PMD dries and emergers ten or fifteen times for every time I've fished a PMD nymph.

I've indulged my PMD dry-fly and emerger habit on a whole lot of rivers in Washington, Montana, Colorado, and a few other states. I love dropping a Morris Emerger, PMD, among those elegant drifting mayflies and the trout working them.

Along the way I discovered that although there's a quality of sunshine in the yellowy wings and bodies of PMD duns, that's about the sunshine limit for these little buggers—they're no fans of bright, clear skies. Yes, they'll show under a naked sun, but then their hatching tends to be brief. Give them a layer of clouds overhead and they'll come off for hours. I remember fondly an Idaho cutthroat-trout river running heavy under fluctuating rain. The PMDs started every morning and paraded through raindrops and the noses of trout steadily into late afternoon. After three great days of fishing, the rain stopped. The remaining two days of the trip were tough fishing to overfed trout with too few mayflies coming off to matter. A few years later on a day of little storms swept through in succession by strong winds, I watched PMDs on a small Montana tailwater hatch to the delight of brown trout whenever clouds cut off the sun. But they halted their hatching altogether each time the sun appeared. It went back and forth like that all afternoon. Each storm was worth the waiting.

According to my fellow author Dave Hughes, in his book, *Pocketguide to Western Hatches*, PMD "duns emerge in the surface film or just beneath it." Dave

knows far more about entomology than I, so I'll take his word. Besides, that fits with my experience. Duns that hatch below the film would logically call for dead-drift wet flies. Duns that hatch in the film call for a standard emerger. Ever since I got the fly right several years ago, I've been reaching for my Morris Emerger, PMD, whenever I see the duns coming off—it's proven itself on difficult rainbows and browns in rivers around the West. The fly holds its wing high, so it's easy to spot on the water, and it floats with unusual determination for a half-sunken emerger fly. But many fly fishers fish Compara-duns and Quigley Cripples during PMD hatches with no complaints and catch plenty of trout on them.

The process of fishing an emerger or dry fly during a PMD hatch is straightforward: Drop the fly well upstream of a rising trout with enough slack in line, leader, and tippet so that the fly drifts freely and naturally. Often easier said than done, of course. Because PMDs live in and hatch from water sometimes lazy slow (though they also like currents up to medium-quick), some trout can get plenty of time to inspect your imitation for size, shape, color, and behavior. Therefore, your slack-line casting must be good, to provide a long, convincing drift of the fly. Accurate too, since PMDs often hatch in considerable abundance, which allows a trout to confine its feeding within a small area and just take in the feast.

Lots of sedate little insects on slow currents can make trout difficult to catch. The increasingly popular solution to tough rising trout is the downstream presentation. It's a great way to get an excellent drift of the fly without spooking the fish with your fly line. Sometimes it's the only solution.

The subsurface emergence of some PMDs presents a facet of mayfly fishing that seems largely ignored. Here, a wet fly, dead-drift, perhaps as a dropper off a dry fly that serves as an indicator, makes sense. It's easy to imagine a trout snubbing dry flies and half-sunken emerger flies while moving to another helpless mayfly struggling toward the surface, hampered by broad wings. I've looked into a clear river during a PMD hatch to see the wink of tiny wings below the surface. I used to wonder what that was about.

**Below:** Flat-water PMDs and angler-wise brown trout—tricky, tricky . . . CAROL ANN MORRIS

## Scan to watch Video:
## Favorite PMD Patterns

Trout focused on underwater-hatching PMDs seems a worthy subject for study and experimentation. I haven't pursued that yet, but it's on my list.

The spinner stage deserves exploration too, and God knows I've tried, but Fate seems to prefer I stay out of that business. I know there are good PMD spinnerfalls, and I have caught evening-rise trout on PMD spinner flies. But I've never really hit it right. Three years ago on a lazy Montana tailwater river I was ready. Everything seemed perfect: PMDs hatching all day, and according to local knowledge, they'd been doing so for a few weeks; every hank of water-weed crawling with PMD nymphs; an ideal slick where I knew the browns loved to rise when the sun set. I was prepared with the right flies and the rest. And I caught some good fish, on a PMD spinner fly in fact, but the spinners never showed in serious numbers. A nasty storm drifted through with lightning and a downpour, and that seemed to put the spinners off. It didn't put off the trout though, nor me. But even after the storm passed and things settled, few spinners came and the trout had to settle for those and a spare mix of a few other various insects. Later that week, same thing: good hatch all day, waiting at the slick, thunderstorm. See what I mean? Fate.

I will attend a real big-time PMD spinnerfall. Persistence will pay off. Someday. Once it finally happens, it'll probably happen all the time after that. I've seen things go that way before.

I have to tell you about my favorite PMD fishing—it's when PMDs work in harmony with Western Green Drakes. Spring through early summer is when I usually catch this mayfly tag-team event. When I do catch it, I gener-

ally keep going back to it. There may be other rivers, other fish, other hatches nearby, but I'm not about to miss a PMD and Green Drake day for almost anything. I've seen it in Montana. I've seen it in Idaho. Even a little in Oregon.

The PMDs come off for hours under clouds, and as their hatch tapers off, the Drakes start to show. The Drakes are no better than the PMDs—the trout keep feeding in about the same way, and I haven't noticed particularly larger fish coming up. But switching from one mayfly to another is a pleasant change. Bigger flies that are easier to see in the fading light, the haunting cool and calm of evening . . .

Still, a day of just PMDs all by themselves is something I'm not likely to miss either.

**Note:** Skip's book *Fly Tying Made Clear and Simple* teaches the tying of the Troth Pheasant Tail Nymph and the Compara-dun. His book *Trout Flies for Rivers, Patterns from the West That Work Everywhere* will teach you to tie his Morris Emerger, PMD, through both written instructions (with photos) and video.

**Below:** The author's mood is good almost any time he's fishing, but it always rises like a nymph wriggling toward the water's surface whenever he sees prim, soft-yellow PMD duns, wings and body held high, drifting down the currents. CAROL ANN MORRIS

**TROTH PHEASANT TAIL**

*CAROL ANN MORRIS*

*Al Troth*

| | |
|---|---|
| **Hook:** | #14-18 (for PMDs) heavy wire, standard length to 1X long |
| **Thread:** | Brown 8/0 or 6/0 |
| **Tail:** | Pheasant-tail fibers |
| **Rib:** | Small copper wire |
| **Abdomen:** | Pheasant-tail fibers |
| **Wing Case and Legs:** | Pheasant-tail fibers (one bunch of uncut tips creates both) |
| **Thorax:** | Peacock herl |

**Notes:** Every seasoned fly fisher knows the Pheasant Tail, that is, the Troth Pheasant Tail. The other Pheasant Tail came from Englishman Frank Sawyer. It's a real standard in Europe.

**MORRIS EMERGER, PMD**

*CAROL ANN MORRIS*

*Skip Morris*

| | |
|---|---|
| **Hook:** | #14-18 light wire, humped shank (pupa/emerger hook) |
| **Thread:** | Yellow 8/0 |
| **Tail:** | Brown mottled hen back (hen-saddle) |
| **Rib:** | Fine gold wire |
| **Abdomen:** | Pheasant-tail fibers |
| **Thorax:** | Soft-yellow buoyant dubbing |
| **Wing and Burst Shuck:** | Bleached or natural light coastal deer hair. |

**Notes:** Make a fan of the deer-hair tips, angling forward slightly, and trim the butts straight across over the rear of the thorax. You can adjust the Morris Emerger with alterations mainly in size and colors for nearly all mayfly hatches.

**COMPARA-DUN, PMD**

*CAROL ANN MORRIS*

*Al Caucci and Bob Nastasi*

| | |
|---|---|
| **Hook:** | #14-18 light wire, standard length or 1X long |
| **Thread:** | Olive 8/0 |
| **Tail:** | Blue-dun hackle fibers, split |
| **Body:** | Buoyant olive-yellow dubbing |
| **Wing:** | Natural light or bleached coastal deer hair, the tips forming a fan |

**Notes:** It works. Compara-duns do that.

**LIGHT CAHILL**

*CAROL ANN MORRIS*

*Dan Cahill*

| | |
|---|---|
| **Hook:** | #14-18 light wire, standard length or 1X long |
| **Thread:** | Tan or cream 8/0 |
| **Tail:** | Ginger hackle fibers |
| **Body:** | Buoyant cream dubbing (originally badger underfur) |
| **Wings:** | Lemon wood-duck fibers, upright and divided |
| **Hackle:** | Ginger |

**Notes:** A solid choice for the traditionalist—I used the Light Cahill successfully for years during PMD hatches.

# Summer

Evening light often means fish and bug activity. RICK HAFELE

*Rick Hafele*

# Evening Magic

If there is one thing fly fishers hope for, it's rising trout! No matter what your preferred method of fishing for trout, I've yet to meet a fly fisher who doesn't get excited when a trout's nose breaks the surface to suck in a little fly, or who doesn't sense something primeval when the dorsal fin of a big trout humps up through the surface and disappears again. It is one of those "time stands still" moments. But predicting exactly when this magic will occur can be frustrating at best. That's why the evening rise is so special; one can be sure—well almost sure—of rising trout when daylight fades and evening shadows prevail.

Caddis adults swarming above streamside trees before dropping to the water to lay eggs. RICK HAFELE

**Right:** *Hydropsyche*, or net-spinning caddis adult, also called the Spotted Sedge, is a common caddis on summer evenings.
RICK HAFELE

"Crepuscular" is the term given to activities that occur at twilight. Deer are crepuscular when they move from resting to feeding areas just before dark. The sudden appearance of nighthawks as daylight fades to darkness or the flurry of bats over a lake at twilight are other examples of crepuscular behavior. A lot of animals find twilight the perfect time to come out of hiding, apparently finding some measure of safety in the mix of light and darkness. I can imagine trout also feel safer near the water's surface just before darkness falls when predators like osprey or

herons lose the benefit of spotting them in bright light. But besides safety, trout need something to rise for. Fortunately for trout and fly fishers, a lot of insects are crepuscular and thus become quite active at twilight as well. That's the beauty, and frustration, of the evening rise: a lot of insects come out and get trout feeding, but it can be very hard to see what is on the water and what the trout are taking.

A number of years ago I had an evening rise to remember on the Deschutes River in Oregon. The Deschutes is a big river with some very well-fed trout, but on bright, sunny, warm days most stay deep while the sun is on the water. Some trout can be tempted with deeply sunken nymphs, but it's when the final rays of light disappear behind the canyon rim and twilight descends that the river and the trout come alive.

On this particular evening I was at the tailout of a favorite riffle watching carefully for the first caddis adults to start swarming, first over the tops of the nearby juniper trees, then over the tailout in front of me. The caddis began showing up as planned and I quickly knotted on a low-riding caddis dry fly. Right on cue a few rises appeared where bits of foam came together in a current seam. Seemed like this was going to be too easy. However, as you have probably guessed, my caddis pattern went untouched while more trout started rising. What the #@*$? Clearly they were taking something besides caddis.

At that point my attention was drawn to some swallows about 20 feet above the water. It took a while, but I finally saw a group of mayfly spinners silhouetted against the light gray sky. "So spinners must be what those trout are taking," I thought, and promptly changed to a little spinner pattern. You've got it. Once again my fly bounced happily down the riffle so close to rises that the rings knocked my fly sideways half an inch, but not one taker. Now I was getting desperate. In another fifteen or twenty minutes I'd be out of light completely. Luckily I had my pair of small binoculars around my neck. There was still enough light reflecting off the water's surface to get a good look at what was floating downstream not more than 30 feet away from me.

With the binocs I saw caddis adults, mayfly spinners, a small stonefly adult, and tucked among them all little size 22 midge adults by the hundreds, drifting and often disappearing in a trout's mouth. I was amazed that all the other insects kept drifting by untouched. It was like an all-you-can-eat buffet where nothing was touched but the sunflower seeds.

Well, I may have arrived at the party late, but after tying on a little Griffith's Gnat I finally felt that wonderful throb of a hefty trout heading out into heavy current. Now all I had to do was avoid breaking the 6X tippet.

**Below:** Trout can be found eating a variety of food in the evening, but midges, both adults and pupae, are often at the top of their menu. RICK HAFELE

Mayfly spinners end up dead on the water with their wings straight out and flat on the water. This makes them very difficult to see any time of day, but especially late in the evening. The mating swarms above the water, however, can be relatively easy to see silhouetted against the evening sky. When you see such swarms, always be on the lookout for trout taking spinners on the water. RICK HAFELE

*Rick Hafele*

when you are faced with picky trout look closely at the size of the fly on the water compared to the one on the end of your tippet.

- Finally, there's nothing like the pressure of knowing you only have an hour or so to figure it all out before the bugs disappear and the trout stop rising. What to do?

While the evening rise is a common phenomenon, it doesn't typically occur year round. In most places it becomes consistent during the summer, from say late June through early September, when daytime temperatures are high and insect activity, with the exception of terrestrials, is often sparse midday. Once air temperature starts dropping and the bright sun disappears, however, a variety of aquatic insects get active.

Caddisflies are one of the most consistent and important players in this late-evening food fest. Not only do mated females return to lay their eggs, but also many species emerge under the cover of fading light to avoid the mouths of swallows and other birds. In addition, many, if not most, of the female caddis laying eggs on summer evenings dive underwater and swim to the stream bottom to deposit their eggs and then drift back slowly to the surface where they die. This means a diving caddis adult pattern of the proper size can be critical. There are some good patterns created just for this purpose, but in a pinch fishing an Elk Hair Caddis below the surface can work just as well. You'll need a split shot 15 to 18 inches up from your fly so it will sink deep enough and quickly enough. Fish it to rising trout with a down-and-across presentation. Just make sure you let the fish set the hook when it hits. A hard strike on a tight line below you almost always translates into a lost fly and fish. This one step of sinking your dry caddis pattern below the surface will often completely change your success when caddis swarm in the evening and your dry fly is ignored.

Because caddis also emerge in the evening, you might find you need a caddis pupa pattern. Hopefully you know what size pattern you should use. When in doubt, a size 16 or 14 pupa will often be close. In all likelihood you'll still see rising trout when they are taking pupae; however, the rises will be swirls more than classic surface rises. Bottom line: Make sure you have a selection of caddis patterns when you fish the evening rise.

The above scenario illustrates a number of factors that come into play during many evening-rise situations.

- More than one insect will commonly be abundant during that magic hour before dark.
- Trout can be just as selective in near darkness as they are at midday.
- It can be difficult for anglers to see what's on the water, let alone what the trout are actually taking.
- Because of the poor light, the color of your pattern isn't as critical in the evening, but matching size is just as important as during the day. So

# Rick Hafele

Once the sun goes down, expect to see insect activity suddenly pick up and trout responding. RICK HAFELE

Another common and important evening insect is the mayfly spinner. Spinnerfalls create some fantastic dry-fly fishing, but unfortunately many anglers fail to recognize when they are on the water. Because spent spinners lie motionless with their wings out flat on the water, they can be difficult to see. This plus the fact that many are quite small makes them almost invisible from an angler's point of view. But from a trout's point of view, looking up against the sky, even tiny spinners show up like little points of light.

Spinnerfalls occur when females land on the water to lay their eggs shortly after mating in the air. While the dead spinners are a challenge to see on the water, the large aerial swarms of mating males and females are much easier to spot. Look for their characteristic up-and-down dance 10 to 50 feet above the water. During the cool months of the year, mating swarms tend to form in the late afternoon. But during

warm weather, spinnerfalls most often occur at twilight. This makes it even harder to see the spinners on the water, but again you can usually spot the mating swarms in the sky.

Whenever you see a large number of spinners in the air, you can bet that fifteen to twenty minutes later there will be spent spinners on the water. Trout take spinners with quiet little sipping rises that are also hard to spot in the fading light of evening. Watch the water carefully, especially where the current forms small eddies and seams that concentrate whatever happens to be floating on the surface. Pattern size will again be most important in picking the right

**Opposite page:** You might see midge adults swarming over streamside grasses, but more often they float by undetected. RICK HAFELE

# Rick Hafele

fly. You'll also need a good presentation with no drag to fool selective trout taking spinners. If you're struggling with drag, try using a longer tippet, maybe 3 or even 4 feet long if it's not windy. This will add some slack in you leader and allow the fly to drift more freely—at least in theory.

Last but not least, midges provide the third and often most frustrating piece of the evening rise. Midges belong to the order Diptera and the family Chironomidae, often called "chironomids" by anglers. There are literally thousands of species of midges, and though a few may be as large as size 12, the vast majority of species fall into the size 18 to 24 range. These little guys can be hard to see in good light, let alone the minimal light conditions just before dark.

I've been fooled enough times by trout taking midges instead of much more obvious fare that I always suspect them when I'm being toyed with by rising trout. The good news is that complicated patterns are rarely needed. The Griffith's Gnat is a simple fly that rarely fails to work when trout are taking adult midges on the surface. But just as often trout are feeding on midge pupae hanging in or just below the surface film, or on midges struggling to escape their pupal skins flush on the surface. It is almost impossible to tell what stage the trout are focusing on, so I most often start with a dry fly like the Griffith's Gnat, and then if that fails I switch to a pupa pattern or a surface emerger pattern. A drag-free presentation will again be your best friend, and because the flies are so small, don't expect to see them on the water. Watch the area where your fly should be for a rise, or fish your midge pattern off a dropper tied to a larger dry fly, which acts as your strike indicator. It can be challenging but more than exciting when a really large trout sips your tiny size 22 midge off the surface and jumps into the sunset.

**SIMPLE CADDIS**

*Rick Hafele*

| | |
|---|---|
| **Hook:** | #12-18 dry-fly hook |
| **Thread:** | Brown 8/0 |
| **Rib:** | Fine gold wire (optional) |
| **Body:** | Dark brown, gray, or olive dry-fly dubbing |
| **Wing:** | Small bunch of brown or gray CDC fibers tied in over abdomen in shape of caddisfly wing |

**Notes:** This simple pattern floats low on the water, matching the look of many caddis adults on the surface just before dark. You can also fish it below the surface to effectively match adults diving underwater to lay eggs.

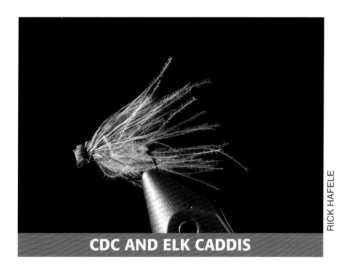

**CDC AND ELK CADDIS**

| | |
|---|---|
| **Hook:** | #12-18 dry-fly hook |
| **Thread:** | Brown 8/0 |
| **Body:** | CDC feather tied in at bend of hook and wrapped up hook shank creating body and long, loose fibers |
| **Wing:** | Deer hair tied in over abdomen |

**Notes:** This fly is described in detail in the book *Tying Dry Flies* by Jay Nichols. I'd recommend you check it out, as it describes many other useful dry-fly patterns besides this one.

**SOFT-HACKLE OR FLYMPH**

| | |
|---|---|
| **Hook:** | #12-18 dry-fly hook 18-12 |
| **Thread:** | Brown or olive 8/0 |
| **Rib:** | Fine gold wire |
| **Body:** | Brown, gray, or olive dubbing |
| **Hackle:** | Partridge body feather or other soft-hackle like hen hackle or quail |

**Notes:** The soft-hackle fly is a pattern that can imitate many different insects, but it is perhaps best suited as a caddis imitation for either a pupa or wet adult.

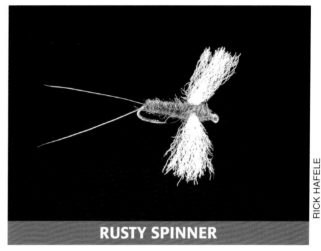

**RUSTY SPINNER**

| | |
|---|---|
| **Hook:** | #12-18 dry-fly hook 18-12 |
| **Thread:** | Brown 8/0 |
| **Tail:** | Two tail fibers tied in divided |
| **Body:** | Dry-fly dubbing to match natural |
| **Wing:** | White poly yarn tied in at right angles to thorax |

**Notes:** I'd recommend always having a fly box filled with spinner patterns of various sizes and colors. The most common color for the female mayfly spinner is a rusty brown. At a minimum carry a supply of the rusty spinner in sizes 18 to 12.

When the sun sets and light gets low many kinds of
insects come out to cavort, and trout materialize from
nowhere to show their appreciation of all the activity.
DAVE HUGHES

*Dave Hughes*

# Patterns and Tactics for the Evening Rise

## Things Aren't Always What They Seem

The single constant that cuts across evening rises is seemingly abrupt change. Trout are doing one thing, you've figured it out, and you're catching them fine. Then suddenly what you've been doing ceases to work, and on account of accumulating darkness, it's almost impossible to figure out what has happened and what to do about it. Close observation is almost always the key to successfully solving these situations.

# Dave Hughes

One of my favorite evening rises happens almost nightly in spring and early summer on one of my favorite high-desert ponds. The pond is small, isolated, largely unknown, and therefore ignored. It contains some big trout, which makes its problems well worth trying to solve. The first time I encountered this particular evening rise, light had dwindled to a dim reflection of a red sky on the pond's surface, where all sorts of mayhem was happening.

I'd been doing fine all afternoon, fishing midge pupa patterns, specifically size 14 Zebra Midges suspended about a foot beneath chartreuse yarn indicators—I use the plural not because I fished the flies in pairs, but because the big trout cleaned me out so often that I ran through a dozen or so of those slender flies, tied to fragile 6X tippets, before evening came slowly on and the trout suddenly wouldn't have anything to do with anything suspended.

I ran through the usual frantic litany of changes and then suddenly realized I was out there to enjoy myself, not flagellate myself. So I sat down on the bank of the pond, in the near darkness, and discovered I was in one of the most beautiful settings in the world. The sun had set behind the distant Cascade Mountains, outlined them starkly, blackly, from behind. The sky had turned as black as the silhouettes of those upthrust mountains. A patchwork of high clouds caught by the settled sun, and ignited red by it, reflected off the water, and gave the surface what little light it had left.

The main defining things I noticed on that still surface were almost continual black noses poking out of the water, sipping something. I had my constant binoculars, so I aimed them out among the rises, just to get a closer view of those trout. What I was able to see through them informed my fishing the next evening, and for a lot of evenings, on a lot of ponds and lakes, ever since.

The surface was covered with small, dark midge adults, swirling, scooting, stopping to sit still, like

**Right:** Many more complicated flies have been tied to match buzzers, but I've found that by adding an extra hackle palmered over the body of an Adams, I'm able to skate the fly, in imitation of the behavior of the naturals. DAVE HUGHES

Midge adults are called "buzzers" in Britain, for good reason. When the sun sets, they land on the water, rev up their wings, and take off buzzing over the surface.
DAVE HUGHES

Don't make the mistake of leaving your favorite stillwater, whether pond or lake, before the sun sets. Midge adults start buzzing around on the surface, and trout give chase and get foolish about flies that are scooted a bit then allowed to sit. DAVE HUGHES

size 16 balls of cottonwood fluff blown about on a breeze, only the pond was windless. British call them "buzzers," and it's easy to see why: their wings whizz, and they buzz along, right on the surface, sometimes leaving soft V-wakes that draw up much larger Vs made by trout calculating their trajectories. Without binoculars, I could see the trout, but not what they were taking. With binoculars, I could follow the flight of a single midge, etched against the slightly red-shining surface, among hundreds or thousands of its kind, until its adventure got punctuated by a black nose arisen.

It was too late to do anything about it that evening. The next day, before hitting the pond with the usual, and as usual successful, suspended midge

pupae, I set up the portable tying vise in the tent trailer and tied a half dozen size 16 Adams, but with extra hackles palmered over their bodies to aid in the buzz.

When the same set of beautiful evening conditions arrived, and the same trout suddenly disdained my pupa patterns, I switched to a long tippet and one of the buzzers. I began calculating the trajectories of the trout themselves: plotting the direction of their rises as they set their sights on the buzzing midge adults: one rise, two rises, set the fly where the next would be. I'd draw the fly a foot over the surface, then drop the rod tip, and let the fly sit still.

Satisfyingly often, that plotted third rise would occur, and the reflective surface of the pond would be destroyed by the cavorting of a trout. I took one throat pump sample before quitting, from a 3-pound rainbow, squirted the contents into a vial filled with alcohol. When I examined it in the light of the next day, the dividing line in the trout's feeding pattern was clearly defined. It contained perhaps two dozen midge pupae, in states of digestion from almost pulp to fairly fresh. It also held a dozen or so midge adults, all perfectly preserved—all freshly taken by the trout before I caught it, robbed it of its dinner, and pickled those midges in alcohol. It was easy to see almost the near-night moment at which the trout had turned its attention from pupae to adults.

Another puzzling evening rise happens on the Deschutes River in late June and on into July and even August. You've fished those quiet nights when the wind has finally dropped to nothing and the air is filled with caddis adults. They buzz around, so many of them chasing each other's tails that they form halos in the air over treetops, above sagebrush tops.

Just as many of them fly out over the water, and it's easy to see they're getting onto it, and trout are rising to take them. You know enough about entomology to know they're *Hydropsyche*, Spotted Sedges, and that a size 14 or 16 Elk Hair Caddis is the perfect match for them. In fact, like me, you've been fishing the edges all day with just that fly and have been doing very well with it.

But evening comes on, and the Elk Hair suddenly ceases to interest trout. Those splashy rises, it turns out, are indications of subsurface feeding, not feeding on top.

The caddis adults belong to a brand that lays its eggs under the water. They fly above the water, usually where it's somewhat calm, then they dive, poke themselves through the surface, and begin stroking toward the bottom to get a grasp on rocks or logs down there and then to hold on and patiently deposit their eggs. Trout are acutely aware of what's going on. They hold high in the mild currents and take the

Spotted Sedge adults, in the genus *Hydropsyche*, lay their eggs by swimming down to the bottom. When they're out in great numbers, usually at evening, you will often do better with a sunk fly than you will with a floating imitation. DAVE HUGHES

**Right:** At times, Spotted Sedge pupae get into the evening mix. When they do, trout will feed on adults diving down to lay their eggs and on pupae rising up for emergence, both at the same time. DAVE HUGHES

You can match diving, egg-laying Spotted Sedges with a Hare's Ear wet fly (left), or try either a roughly tied Gold-Ribbed Hare's Ear (center) or Beadhead Hare's Ear Pupa (right) when trout are feeding on both adults and pupae.
DAVE HUGHES

diving caddis adults so near the surface that their rises break through to the top. It looks like they're taking the adults dry.

They're not.

It's also not clear that this adult activity stands alone. Many times, it seems to be mixed in with an emergence of pupae of the same species. I'm not certain of this, because I've never ceased casting long enough to take a throat sample during fishing that is so good.

The solution can be as simple as suspending a wet fly or pupal pattern right off the stern of the dry fly you've been fishing, on about 18 inches of 4X or 5X tippet. That way you're offering trout a choice, and you can easily see which fly they prefer. It also lets you determine exactly when the switch in interest occurs, from the surface to the area just beneath it.

I've had better fishing by removing the dry fly, replacing it with a wet or nymph, and fishing the subsurface fly on a very slow mended swing. That might reflect my preference for fishing old-fashioned wets, however, and also for fishing with the mini-

mum number of trinkets, such as strike indicators and split shot, on my leader. I'm not opposed to any of that; it's just that if I can avoid it and still catch what I consider my share of trout, I'm happier without them. So I often swing a size 12 to 16 Hare's Ear winged wet fly, as an imitation of the swimming adults, or a size 14 to 16 Gold-Ribbed Hare's Ear nymph, as an imitation of the rising pupae. I've never found myself doing poorly if I switch to a size 14 or 16 Beadhead Hare's Ear Pupa.

The key, in the face of this evening switch in the trout's attention from surface fare to sunk stages of the same insect, is to switch yourself: from floating flies to those that sink and swim.

Another difficult evening rise happened to me the first time on Fall River, a spring creek in central Oregon that flows through dense stands of jack pines. It was a warm midsummer day, and various mayflies had been coming off almost all day. Trout would focus on a few Lesser Green Drakes, and I'd use a size 14 Olive Quigley Cripple to catch a few of them. Then they'd switch to a scattering of Pale Morning

# Dave Hughes

Duns, and it was easy to read the situation, change to a size 16 PMD Compara-dun, and catch a scattering more. In the afternoon, a scant hatch of size 20 BWOs prodded a few trout into rising. It was not an easy situation to solve because the naturals were so few and so small and the trout rising to them so careful and concealed in their sipping. But the duns were visible, and it was not difficult to match them with a tiny Olive Cut-Wing Parachute. A scant few trout were happy about that.

Then it became evening, and the game abruptly changed. All the duns were gone, but the trout continued rising. It was in a strange pattern, and I couldn't fathom it, nor could I see anything on the water to prompt it, until I realized a flurry of rises would erupt quickly every time a breeze wafted through the pines, and then subside a few minutes after the wind died down.

I stopped fishing, lay on my belly, and peered over the edge of a grassy bank onto a long flat beneath a stand of trees. It took no time at all to notice a few trout rising the length of the flat, but a long time to notice that they were taking tiny bark beetles awash in the surface film. Then it all made sense. A wind would hit the trees. The branches would sway. A cascade of the beetles would fall to the water. The trout would feed on them eagerly, but with the tiniest of sipping rises. When they'd cleaned the beetles up, the rises would cease and would not begin again until the next breeze batted the trees and delivered new provisions.

I tied on a size 20 Black Crowe Beetle, tied with dyed deer hair, and began fooling a few of the trout in the failing light. But it was impossible to see the fly on the water, and after a fish or two the cranky fly would be impossible to keep afloat, and I'd have to

These bark beetles came out of a trout's stomach. Beetles frequently get blown out of trees and onto the water, most often at evening. If you can't discover what trout are taking, suspect beetles. RICK HAFELE

**Right:** A Black Crowe Beetle (left) or a higher-floating and more visible Black Foam Beetle (right) will almost always fool trout when they're taking beetles, and for some mysterious reason, almost as often when they're not. DAVE HUGHES

Many spring creeks flow through conifer forests. Where they do, beetles get blown out of trees and onto the water, most often at evening. If you can't discover what trout are taking, suspect beetles. DAVE HUGHES

change it out. When it became too dark to do that, I was forced to quit. Since then, though, I've switched to the higher-floating Black Foam Beetle, with its little yellow foam marker, and have been able to do better whenever such situations arise.

It's become such a common phenomenon that I now go right to a tiny foam beetle whenever trout sip but I can't see what they're taking. I always suspect beetles.

I also often suspect that the trout are taking something else, heaven knows what, but they're willing to accept a beetle pattern even when that's not near what they're engaged upon. Bad luck for them. If they're willing to take a beetle pattern, I'm more than willing to furnish one.

# The Other Magic Hour

For my wife, Carol, who is both a photographer and a fly fisher, the words "magic hour" carry sweet promise . . . and a touch of frustration. A rich, golden sort of light emerges at the last hour of a clear day, and photographers love it—it casts its glow over everything they shoot. Which is why they graced it with that mystical name. However, at the end of a hot day of sunshine— typically an unproductive day on a trout river—the trout, safe from most predators in the waning light, come up to fill their bellies on the burst of insect activity. In other words, the trout make up for lost time. And there's Carol, the fly-fisher photographer who's forced to choose one of her passions over the other. Tough call. I have no such dilemma. I just go after the fish.

Wonderful things can happen at sunset, and better things can happen after that: few, if any, other anglers, air still, shadowy water with its gently feeding trout. RICK HAFELE

I don't mean to sound unsympathetic, but really, it's not that bad for Carol. Last light is only the start of the fishing action, and the later it gets, the more limited the photographic opportunities become. Typically, she gets in her licks on both accounts.

The fly fisher's version of the magic hour is called the "evening rise," and it starts not long before the photographer's magic hour winds down. Usually, the evening rise lasts twenty to ninety minutes, so it's the *fly fisher's* magic hour. When it goes right, it goes something like this. Shadows lengthen and spread as the sun sinks into the horizon. At some point—it's difficult to say exactly when—it begins: The trout show at the river's surface. Perhaps only a solitary rise at first, maybe in the light swirl beside a quick line of current. Then, minutes later, another rise from another fish in the lazy slick of a tailout. New fish keep appearing here and there. The thing builds, until trout are dimpling the dark water steadily, and if it's really good, they're finally showing about everywhere a trout might feed. A quiet frenzy.

It's often the most intricate and intense and plain best fishing of the whole day. It's also calm, the air peaceful and silent but for the occasional calls of night creatures and perhaps the steady rush and gurgle of the river's quick places.

In my own experience, the more stifling the heat and the slower the fishing through daylight, the better the evening rise. Of course, poor fishing weather is just the kind most people seek—bright and hot. That's OK in chilly spring and fall when fish and insects both wait for the comfort of midday warmth. In already sizzling midsummer, though, late morning through midafternoon is hardly worth the bother of pulling on wading boots. Better to hit the water around sunrise, take a long midday break and an early dinner, and return just before sunset. Sunset, though, is exactly when so many anglers pack up and leave. Oh well, now you know better . . .

Evening isn't the only time you can find trout working the top of a river, of course. On a cloudy, cool day, trout may feed hard even at the top of the

water from morning on through into late afternoon, and by sunset, be done. But each river, each river's trout, and each day on each river, is unique. I've seen midday rivers come alive in sizzling, sunny mid-August with insects on top and trout nosing them down, and on some of the rivers where this occurred, that's the norm.

While it's true that trout feel safer from predators after sunset than during the day, they never feel *truly* safe. And they know—they seem to feel it in their flesh—that feeding at the surface exposes them. So don't expect evening-rise trout to come easily. Yes, they may come easily, but they may instead be a real challenge. For one thing, during the evening rise big dry flies are often ineffective, unless some insect adult that's big—such as the huge October Caddis—is on the water. (Besides, trout slapping down big insects after sunset isn't really the evening rise . . . it's just evening feeding.) Most of the time, expect to toss small to tiny stuff out there—size 16 caddis dry flies, size 18 BWO spinners, size 22 adult midges—on tippets no heavier than 5X. And expect to set your

flies down quietly well upstream from the rises of a trout—a fly dropping down a foot up from a trout holding inches under that smooth surface . . . well, that's one trout gone, and perhaps a few others spooked.

Can't say I've done a lot with nymphs during the evening rise. It seems as though, in such low light, trout are focused on the surface of the water. I suppose it makes sense: A significant amount of the food will lie concentrated on or in that plane that is the face of the water, and it'll be the easiest food to see, silhouetted against whatever faint glow remains in the sky. But there have been exceptions. More than once I've been able to take evening trout only with size 22 and 24 midge pupa imitations suspended just below a fine tippet treated with floatant—nymphs below the water's surface, even if only slightly below it. I suspect the reason that only a sunken nymph sometimes turns the trick where the dry fly and half-floating emerger are normally the solution is that the trout are wary and the tiny suspended nymph is among the most difficult deceptions for trout to see through.

*Scan to watch Video:*
## Three Evening Fly Patterns

But nothing in fishing is certain, thank God! Remember how I said the hot months produce the best evening rises? I recall a dynamite evening rise in October. The day had been chilly, and with the sun's leaving, the air turned downright frigid. Yet on went the trout, stirring the dark water with their gentle feeding. Carol, a friend, and I hooked only a few fish on dry flies and emergers, and in the end I went to a size 22 midge pupa suspended on 7X tippet, dead-drift, and it worked and kept working. As if that's not strange enough—a fine evening rise after a cold day—these were cutthroat trout! Popular wisdom regards cutthroats as pushovers. And that's the problem with popular wisdom in fishing—it can be dead wrong, even if it's usually right. So the evening rise shouldn't have come on that cold October river and those cutthroats shouldn't have required the subtlest of approaches. But they did.

On the other end of this theme, you can have ideal conditions for the evening rise yet wait faithfully as it fails to even begin to happen. I can't count the times. On other occasions, the trout wait until almost dark to show, and then shortly after that, when it's just black everywhere, they quit, leaving you heartbroken after only a quarter hour of action. Such is fishing.

One thing's for sure, a stormy sunset is highly unlikely to produce a decent evening rise.

The insect hatches that draw trout up to feed at the surface of a river are always dicey—you can never really count on hatches—so why, when conditions are right, is the evening rise so reliable? For starters, the evening rise really *isn't* reliable—it's just closer to providing consistent surface action than any other period throughout a day of fishing a trout river. I think the primary fuel behind the evening rise is simply the low light and the sense of freedom this provides the trout—the combination of enough light for feeding but too little light for predators to do their sinister work is considerable motivation, especially after spending several hours shunning the dangers of sunlit surface feeding. Another reason the evening rise is reliable: It comes with sunset, and sunset is

**Below:** An average daytime trout, like this one, is probably about the size of an average evening-rise trout—but the odds of hooking a brute go up as the sun goes down. Be alert when fishing the evening rise so you're ready to play a big trout wisely right from the hookup. You'll need all the advantage you can get in the near-dark. RICK HAFELE

*Scan to watch Video:*
## Tying CDC Spinner Wings

absolutely reliable. When did you last see the sun *not* set? Besides, insects seem to prefer low light as well. The spinners of most mayflies return to the water to oviposit in the evening, caddis adults too, and midges, and many of the stonefly species—there's often plenty on the surface of a river for trout to eat at sundown, and considerable variety.

But that variety of evening-rise insects ranging from minuscule to hefty fails to explain why I so often do best after sunset with tiny flies—18s, 22s, even 24s, occasionally 26s. You'd think that if not only speck-size midges but substantial stoneflies and caddis are drifting by, the trout would take a size 14 no problem. And sometimes they will, but frequently they won't. Generally, it does seem the more cautious trout are during the day, the smaller they want their dinner. But the shift can be alarming. Eager trout that slammed huge garish Chernobyl Ants all day can, in the fading light, suddenly think they're wise, old chalkstream browns and insist on size 22s, perfectly drifted. This doesn't always happen, but it happens often enough that if I'm not getting takes after sunset, I keep going with smaller flies and finer tippets until I do get takes.

Sometimes, though, a size 14 dry fly or emerger takes trout all evening, sometimes even a size 12. Keep an open mind—it's your best defense against evening-rise failure. Any failure, for that matter.

Finding your fly on the dark water of sunset and beyond is a neat trick if the fly's a 14, nearly impossible if it's a size 24—but don't let that keep you away from the fascination of the evening rise. Just use that same skill that leads your eyes to your dry fly 50 feet out on a choppy river in the daytime. In other words, if you've spent much time fishing a dry fly, you know pretty much where the fly is even before you look—it's an ability that comes quickly to the newbie fly fisher simply because he or she spends so much time searching the water for the floating fly. Just apply

that skill—instinct, really—to fishing after sunset. Make the cast, let your gut tell you where the fly is, follow that spot in the current as it drifts along, strike when a trout shows anywhere near it. You'll miss a few fish—so what? You'll land some too.

Since the evening rise is about rising trout, tippets are normally pretty fine. You could reason that the low light will allow for 4X or even 3X, but it doesn't seem to work that way—those calm trout holding just below the surface of the water get a good look at a tippet backlit against the sky's last light. I'll start with 5X if the fly is a size 16 or 18, but if I'm playing with sizes in the 20s, I'll go with 6X. On the toughest evenings, 7X. Perhaps a 9-foot leader with 3 feet of tippet.

Rods, reels, lines? I usually go with whatever I was using through the day. For trout-river fishing, that's often a 6-weight line on a 6-weight rod. Why a 6? Because I may switch from little dry flies to a nymph rig complete with weighted fly and split shot and indicator or maybe even to a streamer on a sinking-tip line in a day's river fishing—a 6-weight outfit can do all that—and do it well. Of course, if you can get your hands on a 4-weight rod and line for the evening rise, makes sense. All in all though, I've found that quiet presentations of the fly are much more about the caster's skill than about line weights.

Get to know the evening rise—and for God's sake don't start packing up to leave when it comes, as so many do. The fly fisher's magic hour (or two, if it starts early, runs late) can save more than a few fishing days. And it's as intriguing and rewarding as fly fishing gets.

**Note:** Skip's book *Trout Flies for Rivers* contains all three of the following patterns and their variations. His book *Fly Tying Made Clear and Simple II: Advanced Techniques* details the tying of the WD 40 and the CDC Biot Spinner.

SKIP MORRIS

## CDC BIOT RUSTY SPINNER

*René Harrop*

**Hook:** #14-20 light wire, standard length to 1X long
**Thread:** Brown 8/0 or 6/0
**Tail:** Light blue dun hackle fibers, split or flared
**Abdomen:** Rust goose biot
**Wings:** Light blue dun CDC, light blue dun Z-Lon or coarse Antron yarn on top
**Thorax:** Rust synthetic dubbing

**Notes:** Many mayfly spinners turn rust color, making this a valuable pattern for the evening rise when tied in a range of sizes.

SKIP MORRIS

## SKADDIS DARK

*Skip Morris*

**Hook:** #8-22 light wire, standard length to 1X long
**Thread:** Brown 8/0 or 6/0
**Abdomen:** Buoyant brown poly dubbing (Fly Rite preferred for sizes 16 and up) or another buoyant synthetic dubbing
**Wing:** Yellow poly yarn over brown poly yarn
**Hackle:** One, brown, spiraled over the thorax
**Thorax:** Same dubbing as in the abdomen

# Skip Morris

**Notes:** For years I've trusted the Skaddis for imitating caddis and small stonefly hatches and for those times when it just seemed right for rising trout (some of those times coming during the evening rise). Another option for the wing is to use a few strands of pearl Krystal Flash under the yarn. Trim the hackle flat or to shallow V underneath for slow water.

SKIP MORRIS

## WD 40

*Mark Engler*

**Hook:** #16-28 light wire, short or standard length, straight or humped shank
**Thread:** Olive-brown 8/0 or finer
**Tail and Wing Case:** Natural light bronze mallard
**Abdomen:** The working thread
**Thorax:** Muskrat (or gray rabbit or synthetic dubbing)

**Notes:** The tail and wing case are one uncut section of bronze mallard, covered by the thread through the abdomen. Imitates both hatching Blue-Winged Olive mayflies and hatching midges.

# Ants for All

It's not a farfetched idea that ants will take over the world. In fact one could reasonably make the case they already have. While beetles win the "who's got the most species" contest, when it comes to sheer numbers and widespread presence ants win hands— or should I say tarsi—down. E. O. Wilson, the renowned population biologist who has studied ants for more than fifty years describes it well in his book, *The Super Organism*:

About 6.6 billion individuals compose *Homo sapiens*, the most social and ecologically successful species in vertebrate history. And the number of ants alive at any given time has been estimated conservatively at 1 million billion to 10 million billion. If this latter estimate is correct, and given that each human weighs on average very roughly 1 or 2 million times as much as a typical ant, then ants and people have (again, very roughly) the same global biomass.

That's a lot of ants!

Ants occur everywhere, but streams or lakes surrounded by trees offer some of the best ant fishing opportunities. And remember, ants may be present even if you don't see any. RICK HAFELE

Besides occurring nearly everywhere, ants are delicious. If you've never tried them you should (well, I think you should). A quick Google search on ant recipes will get you started. For some reason most ants are eaten in countries other than the United States. The eggs of some ants are the key ingredient in a Mexican dish called escamoles. I've read this sells for as much as $40 per pound, apparently due to the difficulty of finding the eggs (you also need a lot to make an omelet) and they are available only at certain times. A variety of other ant dishes are served in India and throughout Asia, and Native Americans were also known to eat them.

If you prefer not to eat ants, then you can always eat what eats ants. And one thing that eats ants any chance it gets is a trout. Trout of all species and sizes love ants. This is not news to most if not all of you, but it bears remembering on those warm summer days when finding a willing trout can be harder than keeping ants out of your kitchen cabinets. And

remember unlike the ants in your kitchen, the ants that trout eat often go unseen by anglers, so even though you see no ants floating downstream or along the lake shore, when everything else has failed you might just want to try one of those ant patterns you tied years ago and placed in that hidden fly box compartment.

There are times when ants are more obvious. This occurs during those annual events when they sprout wings and take to the air. Most of the year queen ants produce eggs that become some type of worker ant or soldier ant, which keep the colony functioning smoothly. These ants are all wingless and sterile and focus solely on their job. But periodically, usually once a year in the late spring or early summer, the queen produces eggs that hatch into ants for a whole different purpose. These ants sprout wings and are a mix of fertile males and females. They too have a single job: fly from the nest, mate, and start a new colony. If you've seen flights of these winged reproductive ants you know how amazing they can be. Literally tens of thousands, or even millions, take to the air over a fairly short period of time, typically just several days. Few of these ants actually complete their mission of starting new colonies. Most find untimely deaths in the mouths of a wide variety of birds and animals. If there is water nearby, thousands may end up floating on the surface, unable to escape. If you happen to be a trout when this happens, you throw caution to the wind and begin a feeding binge on ants. Such an event is often called an "ant fall" by fly fishers.

Fishing an ant fall can be one of the truly great fishing experiences you can have, and should be on every fly fisher's bucket list. Water that seemed devoid of trout, or at least large trout, can suddenly appear to be filled with them. And they are stupid easy to catch. I can't forget such an event on a mountain lake a number of years ago. I'd fished this particular lake many times and knew from experience that it held some respectable trout, but I always had to work for them and often left having caught just one or two small fish. When I arrived on this day in mid-June, nothing seemed different. I didn't see any fish rising, but a light breeze put enough chop on the surface that any subtle rises would go unnoticed. After rigging up, I waddled out in my float tube and began casting a dragonfly nymph in toward some downed logs. After twenty minutes or so without a strike I was debating what to do next, when out of the corner

Ant eggs and pupae—delicious!

A winged carpenter ant like this one can produce some of the best fishing of your life!

**Right:** Carpenter ants are just one of some fourteen thousand species of ants worldwide. Most produce winged adults that mate and spread colonies far and wide. PHOTOS BY RICK HAFELE

Since ants don't live in lakes or streams, they only end up in them by mistake. Thank goodness such mistakes are fairly common.

**Right:** Trout don't grow this fat eating ants, but trout this fat throw caution to the wind when ants are readily available. PHOTOS BY RICK HAFELE

of my eye I caught the flash of a trout near the surface. This got me looking more carefully, and it wasn't long before I saw another flash and a swirl that indicated this trout took something off the surface. About then a fat carpenter ant landed on my float tube. If I could have read it's mind, I'd say it was quite nervous about its situation—trout infested water all around and only a little island of rubber to sit on for safety.

Well, it wasn't hard to put slashing trout and carpenter ant together and decide I better try an ant pattern. After searching through my fly boxes, the best ant pattern I could come up with was a dark brown Deer Hair Caddis that I trimmed to look more antlike. It was one ugly looking ant, but it didn't matter. After tossing my caddis-turned-ant out into the surface chop, I didn't have to wait long before a serious swirl inhaled the fly and a gorgeous 15-inch rainbow headed for deep water. This was repeated a ridiculous number of times, until I finally felt silly and my wrist was aching. That night I tied a dozen real ant patterns and the next day drove—more like sped—back to the lake. Once again it was ant city, and the fish came like mallards to bread. It was a week before I could return to the lake again. When I did the ants were gone, and the trout were back to their normal picky selves.

Such is the world of the ant fall—here one day, gone the next. And it's next to impossible to predict when these ant falls will happen. To me that's the biggest downside to ant falls; trout can't resist them when they are available, but you can't predict when or where ant falls will occur. Generally ant falls occur

sometime in May or June, or depending on elevation and weather conditions maybe July. Later in the year, in August and September, you aren't likely to run into a big fall of winged ants, though late season ant falls do occur. By their nature, ants are always crawling around and frequently—more frequently than you might think—find themselves in the water. Therefore, on a hot summer afternoon, when trout seem to be asleep and the chance of hooking one on a dry fly seems less likely than landing a tarpon with a 6-weight rod, casting an ant pattern out under some overhanging trees or along an undercut grassy bank can change everything.

As I found out years ago, an exact imitation isn't always needed when trout are on to ants. That said, it still makes sense to have some decent ant patterns in your arsenal of terrestrial patterns. I've tried many different styles over the years and have basically settled on a foam ant pattern, both with and without wings to cover flying ants and the more common wingless forms. These patterns float low on the water

**Below:** Late summer can still mean ants are on the trout's menu. If you see rises and nothing on the water, try fishing a low-floating wingless ant pattern. Many times this works even if ants aren't around, and it rarely fails if they are. RICK HAFELE

Pay close attention to areas with overhanging trees. Ants may fall in anytime. RICK HAFELE

Termites (top) resemble ants (bottom), especially when they produce winged reproductive adults. But they are actually very different insects. To trout, however, they both mean reckless feeding when available. RICK HAFELE

and sometimes sink just below the surface. That's fine. Real ants do the same thing. It can make it hard to see your fly on the water, however, so if that's causing problems, tie your ant to a dropper attached to a bigger dry fly, like a grasshopper, for an indicator. This combination can do double duty during the warm summer days.

Natural ants come in a wide range of sizes, but a selection of patterns tied in sizes 16, 14, and 12 will cover the vast majority. As for color, burnt orange, red, or black seem most common.

One last thing: ants vs. termites. Termites and ants are often considered similar by a lot of folks, when they are really quite different insects. Ants belong to the order Hymenoptera (which contains bees, wasps, and ants), and termites belong to the order Isoptera (which contains termites only). While different taxonomically, they do share similarities in size, color, and general shape. They are also both social insects that live in large colonies and both

Trout just can't leave ants alone. RICK HAFELE

produce winged individuals that end up on the water at certain times of the year. And like ants, trout seem to love termites when they are available. Because of their overlap in size and color, if you have a good selection of ant patterns you will probably have a pattern that will work if termites are on the water instead of ants. A big difference between ants and termites is that termites are only available to trout in the winged stage, as worker termites remain well hidden inside wood or underground and do not end up in the water.

A simple foam ant has become my pattern of choice over the years. They can be easily tied in different colors, with or without wings, and in a range of sizes.

**FOAM ANT**

RICK HAFELE

| | |
|---|---|
| **Hook:** | #12-18 standard dry fly |
| **Thread:** | Black 6/0 or 8/0 |
| **Body:** | Closed-cell foam in color of your choice |
| **Wing:** | White or pale tan poly yarn |
| **Legs:** | Light brown hackle |

The author on the sort of coastal stream where he
first learned to drown an occasional black beetle.
RICK HAFELE

# Fun With Beetles

I've had a lot of fun with beetles over many years, some in ways you won't approve. When I first started fishing in the coastal creeks around Astoria, Oregon, where I was born and raised and often wish I still resided, the waters were full of wild trout, the limit was ten, and my parents went after them out of desire to eat them. In our preteen apprenticeship years, my older brothers and I fished with bamboo rods, level fly lines, 4-foot leaders, and gold single-egg hooks beneath a hefty split shot pinched to the leader for weight.

# Dave Hughes

A typical black forest beetle, the kind that falls to streams and gets eaten by trout. DAVE HUGHES

**Right:** The construction of a new generation of beetles is an awkward maneuver that frequently causes the participants to fall off their perches and into the water, where trout have little mercy on them. DAVE HUGHES

This worked fine and served as surprisingly good instruction for the nymph fishing that followed many years later in life. But those tiny eggs were parsed out sparingly by my father, and they were also fragile and failed to stay on the hook. As a consequence, it was common that I ran out of bait about halfway through a fishing day. Early on, I'd get together with one of my brothers and whine until he shared a few of his own remaining eggs, and that, too, became early instruction in the important skill of whining when one of your fishing partners has the right fly, and is whacking the trout, while you don't seem to have anything that will work.

Just as my fishing partners today have learned to drift off when they see me coming, my brothers quickly learned that the sight of me thrashing up the stream toward them was a signal that it was time to flee the scene. So I was soon left to my own devices whenever I ran out of bait.

That unbrotherly abandonment is what turned me to beetles.

I was sitting disconsolate on one of those huge mossy rocks that lined the streams in those days—they still do today; I just fished a couple of them last weekend and discovered that all of those rocks, and a pleasantly surprising number of those trout, are still there—when I saw a big, black beetle clumsily navigating its way through the greenery. My egg jar was empty, and my middle brother was disappearing upstream in the distance, nearly leaving a rooster tail in his wake in his haste to shake me. I captured that beetle by its carapace, turned it upside down, hesitated a moment when it waved its legs imploringly at me, and then impaled it on my golden hook.

A big pool was right at my feet. I didn't even leave my seat in the moss atop that boulder. I lobbed the beetle out, a bit upstream into the current, and let it settle toward the bottom. You know what happened then, and you also know what happened to a minor portion of the streamside beetle population in coming summers. The best part was that my brothers got together and shook their heads at the cessation of my

**Opposite page:** Guide Holden Hughes with a medium-size trout hooked on a big beetle pattern in the small spring creeks of Estancia del Zorro, in Chilean Patagonia. DAVE HUGHES

Dave playing a fish on the Sylvan Dale pond in Colorado, when the wind was breathless and the surface was still . . . except for an occasional rising trout. MASAKO TANI

whining. But they, too, ran out of eggs from time to time. Once, when we all three turned out to be on empty together, I taught them my little beetle trick.

I haven't used it in years, and recommend that you use it yourself only as backup when your supply of single eggs fails.

My more recent beetle enjoyments have not been so deleterious to the beetle population. I use flies to imitate them now, but I haven't forgotten that my earliest beetle fishing was subsurface, so I often fish them sunk rather than floating.

That aligns itself perfectly with the first dressing that I used, the Black Crowe Beetle. It was, and still is, a very realistic tie. It's made of deer hair dyed black, tied in at the hook bend, then drawn forward over deer hair legs, and tied down again at the front, forming a realistic carapace. It's the perfect imitation, but it's so dense that it's difficult to keep afloat. It is my suspicion that this denseness causes it to float, when it will, low and flush in the surface film, mak-

ing it a more realistic imitation of the natural. But if you can't see it, it's difficult to fish it as a dry fly. So I tend to fish it now only when I desire to fish it as a subsurface fly: almost, as it were, as a nymph. I've been known to slip-knot a little yellow yarn indicator 3 to 4 feet up the tippet from it, in part so I can follow its float, if it happens to be floating, and be aware of its approximate location, but also in order to be first to get the news when a trout takes it some scant inches deep.

I've never tried pinching a split shot to my tippet and fishing a beetle imitation deep. That would be reminiscent of some of my earliest fishing, and I don't doubt that it would be effective. I do use the A. P. Black nymph consistently in my small-stream trout fishing today, but I've never made the connection between the black-carapaced imitation and those first beetles that I dunked in coastal hill streams.

The most practical beetle dressing I've found is from Skip Morris's book *Tying Foam Flies*. It's simple, a quick tie, floats well, and because of its yellow yarn built-in indicator, it's easy to see on the water. You can tie a bunch of them in a hurry, so there's really no excuse not to have a row or two of them in your fly box, from size 12 to 18. I've found occasional need for beetles larger or smaller, but those at the core will catch trout for you most often.

I needed the larger ones once, on a trip to Chile, and failed to have them, a mistake I won't make again. But it was an honest mistake. I was going to fish the small spring creeks at Estancia del Zorro, out of Coyhaique, and was told to tie a supply of "big foam beetle dressings." So I did; I tied an extra couple dozen of the largest size I used at the time, the size 12. When I got there, guide Holden Hughes—no relation and fortunately not aware of my reputation as a whiner—peered into my open fly box, shook his head in disdain, and handed me a Black Foam Beetle . . . in size 4. I didn't even have to whine to get it.

---

**Below:** Dave's wife, Masako, playing a beetle-fooled trout under the careful guidance of Chuck Prather, out of Sylvan Dale Guest Ranch in Colorado. DAVE HUGHES

But I quickly lost it to a trout. The big fish was rising in a spring creek pool about 4 feet wide. I crept up behind a clump of bunchgrass, stuck my rod tip over the edge, flipped the size 4 beetle to the water. The subsequent detonation caused me to lose my cool. I yanked one way and the trout yanked the other. It was only about a 6-pounder, but it still managed to part my tippet and gallop away with Holden's big beetle dressing. He was by then successfully guiding my wife, Masako, far enough upstream that I decided to leave them alone, since they were busy catching similar trout. So I tied on one of my "big" size 12 beetles and was able thereafter to entertain some trout between 10 and 12 inches long. I'll never go to Chile again without a supply of truly big beetles: in size 4 and 6.

One of my most entertaining days with beetle dressings was on a tiny farm pond in central Oregon, out in flat wheat country, where the nearest tree in sight is on the slopes of Mt. Hood at binocular range in the long view. The wind gathers its strength on those same distant slopes, huffs across the intervening flatlands gaining speed, and sweeps over the pond so

# Dave Hughes

violently that it sometimes raises whitecaps. My first day of fishing on the trip was ruined by it.

The second day I remembered some lessons I'd gotten in Ireland, in wind drifting from guided boats. I chose my longest rod, 11 feet, and tied a leader to it the same length. I hiked around the pond until my back was to the wind. Then I let the leader go, before selecting a fly pattern, and it whipped straight out, carried at rod height on the wind. This made me realize that any ordinary dry fly would fly like a kite, in other words, float about 10 feet above the water, where all but the most acrobatic trout might have some trouble getting to it. My eyes, roving around my fly box, landed on those same size 12 beetles that had failed so well in Chile. Their compact bodies spoke of weight, just what I was after that windy day on the pond.

I tied one on and let it loose on the driving currents of wind. It towered up into the air and then parachuted down to the surface. By lifting and lowering the rod tip, I was able to make the beetle dance an awkward ballet across the surface. It got interesting when a big nose poked out under it and tried to take it just as it lifted off the surface. I lowered the rod, dropped the beetle back to the surface, and the trout thrashed at it and missed. I lowered the rod again and the trout came and murdered it swiftly. It only weighed about 3 pounds, and I only caught a dozen or so more in the next couple of hours. No other hatches happened that day; the persistent wind drove them down. I also saw no beetles on the water that day. But whenever I desired a bit of entertainment out of the trout, I'd trot out my awkward ballerina, coax her into dancing over the surface, and she'd draw up some of those detonations for me.

I use beetles on stillwaters more than I do on streams. Once in Colorado, fishing with great guide Chuck Prather out of Sylvan Dale Guest Ranch, beetles saved one of those days that are the opposite of the above windy situation.

The air over the beautiful set of ponds on the ranch was breathless. The Rockies seemed to stand right up next to us, the air was so clear. You could reach out and wrap an arm around their shoulders, like pals. The surface of the pond didn't have a wrinkle on it, but it seemed some midges or terrestrials or

RICK HAFELE

Black Crowe Beetle (left) and Black Foam Beetle. DAVE HUGHES

something were stuck in it. Every once in a while something would die in a very small sipping rise, the sort that often speaks of larger trout than you'd think. I had no idea what the trout were taking and probably had no match for it if I did. But in a problem like that, I know the first answer I always reach for: a size 16 Black Foam Beetle. It didn't let me down.

The only problem was with my patience. Because the rises were so scattered and sporadic, there was not much hope to cover active, feeding fish. It was simply a matter of casting my bread—my beetle!— upon the waters and waiting for something to come and find it. The first time one did, I was gazing up at the mountains when Chuck jabbed me in the ribs and said, "You just missed one!"

After a few more jabs like that, Chuck finally convinced me to pay attention to my fly for more than the first few seconds of its idle float. That turned out to be beneficial; from then on I began hooking trout, and none of them were small. The Rockies receded from my attention, and I was able to focus on that beetle dressing afloat out there on the still surface, because I suddenly had the constant feeling that something was about to pounce it . . . and something constantly did.

## BLACK CROWE BEETLE

*John Crowe*

| | |
|---|---|
| **Hook:** | #14-20 fine-wire dry fly |
| **Thread:** | Black 8/0 |
| **Body:** | Black dyed deer hair |
| **Legs:** | Black dyed deer hair |

## BLACK FOAM BEETLE

| | |
|---|---|
| **Hook:** | #4-20 dry fly |
| **Thread:** | Black 6/0 or 8/0 |
| **Body:** | Black closed-cell foam |
| **Legs:** | Moose body hair |
| **Indicator:** | Yellow yarn or foam |

# Five Hopper Lessons

T he two-week fishing trip to Montana was my high school graduation gift, and it really began when I stood on a broad gravel bar of the sadly shrunken Bitterroot River in late summer. The river is legally protected now from such abuse, but back then the draw of agricultural water turned this fine, big river into no more than a modest creek separating two wide strips of sun-baked stone and cobble. Still . . . there were trout.

# Skip Morris

I crept up on a small, lazy pool and tied on the only fly that made any sense to me, the Joe's Hopper, a standard grasshopper imitation back then—hoppers had sprung and flown off everywhere as I'd walked through tall grass to the river.

I didn't really know what to do other than to toss the fly out there and let it drift. So I did that. Then I waited in real doubt as the quiet current drew the fly in what seemed a spiritless drift along a lower edge of the pool. Knowing no better, I kept doing this . . . until something large made a big swirl on the flat water. Minutes later I beached a 2-pound brown trout. I stared down at it in amazement—it was huge by my standards back then, my first Montana trout, my first brown, and my first trout of any kind on a hopper fly. In those days, catch-and-release was a novelty. I killed the fish, opened it up, and found a bellyful of grasshoppers.

A week or so later I showed the same fly to the wizened brown trout of the rich Firehole River in Yellowstone Park. A good fish materialized slowly, cautiously, moving upward, drifted back with the fly for a moment, and then dematerialized down into the dark depths. The Firehole trout were definitely more streetwise than the Bitterroot trout back then. (In my defense, I did land other trout on the Firehole that day, though not on a hopper fly.)

Since then I've fished hoppers on occasion and sometimes with real success. The primary thing I've learned about such fishing is that it happens at a time when, although the grasshoppers are as happy as lottery winners, I'm staving off misery—late summer with its scalding, relentless sunshine, the air rubbing like a hot stone against my skin. I can take it, but I tend to leave it. My hopper-fishing experience, therefore, is ample simply by virtue of many years of fishing trout rivers.

A considerable amount of that experience came just last summer—grasshoppers were everywhere during a two-and-a-half week trip in August to Idaho and another week in early September in Northern California, so I got a sort of refresher course in

**Below:** You have good reason to hope for larger trout than you normally raise to a dry fly . . . if that fly is an imitation grasshopper. CAROL ANN MORRIS

Grasshoppers live up to their name by preferring and thriving in tall grasses. Wherever a trout stream is fringed by grass, chances of mid- to late-summer hopper fishing are high. RICK HAFELE

making the most of the hulking insects on trout streams running from tiny to large.

So that's **lesson number one: Expect hopper fishing during the hottest time of the season.**

Windy days (in mid- to late summer, of course) up the odds of trout seeking grasshoppers. It's logical: the insects hop and fly with little if any understanding of water, so a gust is likely to stir them to flight and then slap them down where trout live. That's not to say that calm days are hopeless—if there are lots of grasshoppers in the grasses that border a river, enough of them may tumble in to get the trout looking for them. Still, wind should stir your hopes.

That's **lesson number two: Wind is best for hopper fishing, but not always required.**

A common trap fly fishers stumble into is doing just what they think they should be doing while failing to consider alternatives—that is, they close their minds and their eyes. That's always perilous in fishing. If you stop looking—or, really, stop *seeing*—stop experimenting, stop hypothesizing, your odds of success descend like that Firehole brown of my teenage Montana adventure. So if conditions are just right for hopper fishing—a hot, clear day in July up into early September; grasshoppers everywhere, right up to the edges of the river; good wind—remember that, in fact, the trout may be focused on something else. Perhaps they're chasing caddis adults back in the shaded water under cut banks and outstretched tree limbs, or waiting for drifting midge pupae, watching the riverbed for mayfly nymphs nervous for their hatching.

**Lesson number three: Look for grasshopper action, especially when conditions are right for it, but never stop looking for other possibilities, especially when grasshopper flies fail.**

To twitch or not to twitch a hopper fly can be a critical decision. Real grasshoppers often do kick

# Skip Morris

CAROL ANN MORRIS

around when they wind up trapped on the surface of the water. The trick lies in making the action you put into your fly natural, convincing . . . rather than tipping the trout off to your impostor. So I tend to try a dead-drift presentation first. If the trout don't buy it, OK, time to give the fly a little action.

When I do twitch a hopper-fly, I focus, trying to make the movement real—watching a grasshopper on the water is a great help. I also experiment. Sometimes a tiny, occasional twitch will do it; other times, more action is required. A strong wind tends to make grasshopper fishing happen; it also tends to rough up the water your imitation rides, which may be enough to give your fly the life it needs without any help from you.

And there's always the splat—smacking the fly down harshly, which is how many hoppers hit the water. Carry this one up your sleeve.

**Lesson number four: Try fishing a grasshopper fly dead-drift, but be quick to give it action if dead-drift fails.**

There are big grasshopper flies, like the Dave's Hopper, which its originator Dave Whitlock often ties

The fly fisher's grasshopper season starts with small juvenile hoppers—nothing wrong with these, anglers and trout agree. So carry smaller hopper flies along with the big ones. RICK HAFELE

on long-shank size 6 hooks, and little grasshopper flies, such as the Letort Hopper, which its originator Ed Shenk ties down to a long shank size 18. The big ones are, of course, for when grasshoppers are fully grown and anything smaller simply fails to look natural. But early in the season, small grasshoppers may abound.

Of course, as with all fishing, experiment. Perhaps today, with tiny immature grasshoppers all around, the trout will want a big Dave's Hopper more than anything else. They're fish. Go figure.

Color varies. Mostly I've seen grasshoppers with yellow bodies. But I've also seen them with tan, cream, and green bodies; I've even heard of orange. Still, it's mainly yellow-bodied grasshopper flies I carry and fish. Trout will often overlook body color if the fly is correct in size and action.

So here's **lesson number five, the final one: Try to match the size and color of the grasshoppers you see, but keep an open mind.**

Now that you know how and when to fish grasshopper flies, pack a few along in your fly boxes, especially when you're fishing rivers from sweltering mid- to late summer. The need for them may well arise.

SKIP MORRIS

### SHENK'S LETORT HOPPER

*Ed Shenk*

| | |
|---|---|
| **Hook:** | #10-16 light to standard wire, 1X to 3X long |
| **Thread:** | Yellow 3/0, 6/0, or 8/0 |
| **Head/Collar:** | Size-A rod thread |
| **Body:** | Yellow buoyant synthetic dubbing |
| **Wing:** | A mottled brown turkey-quill section toughened with artist's fixative or Dave's Flexament |
| **Head and Hair Collar:** | Natural tan-gray deer hair, flared, compressed, and trimmed to shape |

SKIP MORRIS

### DAVE'S HOPPER

*Dave Whitlock*

| | |
|---|---|
| **Hook:** | #6-14 standard or heavy wire, 2X or 3X long |
| **Thread:** | Yellow 3/0, 6/0, or 8/0 |
| **Head/Collar:** | Size-A rod thread |
| **Tail (optional):** | Red elk or deer hair |
| **Butt:** | Yellow poly yarn, doubled |
| **Rib:** | A brown dry-fly hackle, its fibers trimmed short |
| **Wing:** | Mottled-brown turkey-quill section toughened with artist's fixative or Dave's Flexament, over yellow deer hair |
| **Hopping Legs:** | Knotted pheasant-tail fibers or trimmed yellow hackles |
| **Head:** | Natural tan-gray deer hair, flared, compressed, and trimmed to shape |

# Fall

Desert streams typically have rich insect life and can grow big trout, but they all face a common problem—drought and low water. RICK HAFELE

*Rick Hafele*

# Life in Low Water

Streams, and lakes too for that matter, change in specific ways from season to season just as surely as the leaves on the cottonwood trees along their banks. One of those changes is water level. In most cases water levels change more dramatically through the seasons in streams than lakes, thus low water is typically more common in streams. For this reason my discussion here is going to focus on streams and how water level—low water in this case—affects fish and insects. Skip and Dave will discuss how low water changes fishing tactics, equipment, and fly patterns, so I thought I'd focus on how trout and insects have evolved to cope with low water.

Drifting down a stream in a wetsuit with mask and snorkel provides a view of the trout's world impossible to get any other way.

**Right:** Cool water attracts trout like moths to a light when stream temps rise too high for comfort. PHOTOS BY RICK HAFELE

I've always been amazed at the adaptability of stream-dwelling fish and insects. Over the course of a single year they will commonly experience large floods with extended high water, short duration flash floods that occur with unpredictable frequency, freezing temperatures, muddy water, warm or even hot temperatures, and very low water. To thrive in this type of environment you have to have some good strategies to handle a wide range of conditions. The one thing that doesn't change with perennial flowing streams or rivers, unless man-made changes have significantly changed water flow, is that water continues to flow down their channels for hundreds, thousands, tens of thousands, or even millions of years without interruption. Except for the largest of lakes like the Great Lakes, such permanence is rare for lakes. Therefore, while life in streams has to be able to live in a highly changeable environment, the streams they live in have existed for millions of years, giving the life within them ample time to evolve effective ways to cope with the extreme range of natural conditions.

Many of the changes that occur during low water are obvious, while others are more subtle. Perhaps most obvious is that during low water streams and rivers are smaller. For trout, this means there is less living space, and they have to compete for the best water. This can result in many more trout than good lies, which ties in with Dave's discussion of how trout end up "sprinkled" across a stream during low water and often hold near the banks. For the angler it can mean good holding water will be easier to identify and thus find trout, plus it will be simpler to wade to where you want to fish. Caution and stealth are a must, though, when approaching potential trout

**Below:** Net-spinning caddis larvae become concentrated in the best habitat when low water reduces their available living area. RICK HAFELE

lies during low water if you want more than to just see the quick flash of a trout as it darts away.

Another effect of low water on trout that's less obvious is the rise in water temperature that usually accompanies later summer and early fall drops in flow. You can check this easily enough with a thermometer wherever you are fishing. In most regions and for most species of trout (some unique exceptions do occur), trout find water around 65 degrees tolerable, but they prefer it cooler, with temps in the 50- to 60-degree range nearly ideal. When temperatures range from say 68 to 70, trout start getting uncomfortable. When it rises above 72 degrees, they are downright stressed and will do almost anything to find and hold in cooler water, even if it means being crowded together in a small area or holding in areas with little food. I have observed this firsthand while snorkeling in streams where water temperatures rise to dangerous levels. On more than one occasion I've floated through hundreds of feet of a stream channel without seeing a single trout, only to find fifteen or twenty trout all crowded together in a tight little ball in a small pocket where cool groundwater seeped

into the stream bottom. When approached I could put my hand right into the middle of these trout before they would budge from their little pocket of cool water. And once I left they immediately returned to their little refuge of coolness.

The above example is from a stream where water temps rose to 75 degrees and higher late in the summer, a rather extreme case of high water temperature for a trout stream. But it does point out how trout will move to areas where temperature is more suitable if needed. So if water temperature gets above 65 or 68 degrees and you know areas where cool water enters the stream, either from little springs, groundwater, or cold tribs, you will likely find trout concentrated around these cool water sources. Use your thermometer to check where these areas might be.

You've also probably noticed how lazy you get, and how little you feel like eating, when it's 100 degrees outside. Trout act the same way when water temp gets to 68 or 70 and higher. This means that trout will feed most actively in the early morning, when water temperature is coldest during warm, low-water conditions. Thus early morning may be your best time to catch trout when faced with warm water in trout streams. This doesn't mean a grasshopper pattern fished midday won't bring up some nice trout, even on a hot summer afternoon. But it does mean you will do better fishing that hopper pattern where the water temp is 65 degrees versus 70.

What about aquatic insects and low water? As you probably guessed, there are a whole range of ways aquatic insects deal with low, and warm, water. First, many species of insects anglers routinely imitate are in either the egg stage or have just hatched from eggs and are really tiny nymphs and larvae during the late summer and early fall. I've mentioned before that August and September are typically the low point in aquatic insect numbers in most trout streams. But the insects that are active in streams during late summer and fall low-water periods will be crowded into less living space just like trout. As a result, while the total number of insects in a stream may be low, the number per square foot or square meter may not show a drop at all and could even increase. To a trout this means it will see about the same number of insects drifting by per area of available habitat. And to the angler it means you will be just as effective drifting a nymph or emerger downstream that matches the dominant insect trout are seeing and feeding on.

This leads right into the topic of insect drift and how stream flow affects it. Like most things related to insects the answer isn't straightforward. First, lower flows mean lower current velocities, which means individual nymphs or larvae are less likely to get washed into the drift. Generally the total number of insects in the drift will be lower during low flows. But, again, the number drifting per cubic foot or cubic meter of stream may not be much lower due to the smaller volume of water in the stream channel.

**Below:** Cool water often flows just below the surface of stream-bottom gravel and cobble, a place small nymphs and larvae can readily access when needed. RICK HAFELE

Trout will be looking for shade and cool water during the hot, low-water days of late summer. Smart anglers will be, too. RICK HAFELE

And just like other seasons of the year, insect drift numbers still peak during the hour or two right around sunrise and again around sunset. Because the morning drift peak also corresponds with cooler morning stream temperatures, this can be a great time to be on the water fishing nymphs and other subsurface patterns.

Aquatic insects are overall less affected by warm water temperature than trout. For example, studies looking at the thermal tolerance of a variety of aquatic insects show that most have a higher temperature tolerance than trout. Also, because aquatic insects are small and live in the small spaces on and in between stream bottom rocks, when needed they can often find cooler water in the area under cobbles and boulders. Many species will even clamber down below the surface of the streambed gravels several inches to several feet. This region of the stream bottom is called the "hyporheic zone." During late-season warm-water periods, water temperature in the hyporheic zone can be 4 or 5 or more degrees cooler than the water in the stream channel. In addition, besides a refuge during summer and fall low flows, the hyporheic zone is also a place insects survive floods. There is no question that being tiny has some advantages. The one big disadvantage is that you are on the menu of nearly every other animal under and above the water.

So what's the take-home message here? First, think about how trout have to deal with less living space and where they may go to find cooler water temperature. Second, while aquatic insect numbers are generally low this time of year, the number per stream area is not necessarily low. Finally, you can appreciate the fact that trout and insects live in a changeable environment and are extremely adept at finding ways to thrive in it. It's probably also worth going to Dave's and Skip's chapters to learn how to alter your fishing tactics and gear for these low-water days of late summer and fall.

When the water is down even a bit and trout move to the edges to take advantage of terrestrials falling from streamside vegetation, you need to focus your attention there unless something else—like rising trout—attracts it elsewhere.
MASAKO TANI

*Dave Hughes*

# Low Water
## Nibbling at the Edges

I t's counterintuitive: You'd think trout in low water would be down in whatever depths are left, cryptic and in pods, hiding out and saving energy until flows liven up and things get generally better. But they're not, especially in small to medium-size trout streams. They're more often sprinkled in minor holding lies along the edges and even on shallow tailouts, wherever they can find some slight concealment from predators and shade from the sun.

It's often better to fish from shore when fishing for trout along the banks—wading in and splashing about is a quick way to send cautious trout running for cover. DAVE HUGHES

It makes a bit of sense. Waters become low and clear long after snowmelt has ended, rains have diminished, and ground water has dried to a trickle. That coincides with the end of most aquatic insect hatches and the advent of terrestrial time. Where do those adventurous land insects make the mistakes that get them onto water and into the eyes of trout? Along the edges. When they become the dominant groceries, trout move out of the depths and take what shelter they can find where they're most likely to get fed. They nibble at ants, beetles, grasshoppers, crickets, inchworms, whatever else falls to the water. You should adjust your tactics to nibble at the same edges to get into contact with those trout.

The first part of it is reading the water to find the fish. Trout need three things to be satisfied with their lies: food, shelter from currents, and protection from predators. Food, in the form of all those terrestrials dropping in, is what draws them to the edges. Shelter from fast flows is inherent in times of low water, near the banks; there is not much current to escape. The

friction of water flowing along the edge itself slows the water . . . it's why trout are often tucked so tight there; the water is slowest there. As a consequence of the abundance of food and patience of the currents, protection from predators becomes the need that defines the lies in which you'll find trout along the edges.

What are those predators, and from which direction do they attack? They're kingfishers, osprey, and herons for the most part, and they launch their strikes from overhead. Of course there are also mink, otters, and even us, but we're all more dangerous when trout are podded up than we are when they're sprinkled, so its aerial predation against which trout array their defenses, and choose their lies, along the skinny edges. Which brings up an aside: Trout holding in comparatively shallow lies, as they will be along the banks, are always scattered, usually one per lie, sometimes two if it's a large lie, rarely three. When they're holding in larger, deeper pools, they often pod up. This dictates, in large part, the speed with which you fish banks, as opposed to pools: you move right along, take five casts or ten to a promising spot, make sure you've given every trout in there a chance to ponder your fly, decide whether to whack it. Then you move on to the next lie.

If you hook one, repeat the cast, and hope for another, but based on dispersion rules, if you've hooked one, you're less likely to hook another on a cast to the same place. If you do continue hooking trout from a large lie along the edges, you'll usually catch the biggest one first, then they'll diminish in size. So your pace, along the edges, is much more brisk than it is when you fish the central regions of the stream, where it can be quite wise to linger over a pool and keep casting after you've already caught one to a bunch of trout. Keep pestering the pool until you wear it out. End of aside.

Favorable lies at the shallow edges are defined by three things: depth, darkness, and overhead concealment. If you're hiking along the banks of a river when the water is low and notice any water near the

bank that is deeper than the water upstream and down from it, be sure to fish it. Trout, sometimes two or even three, are sure to be there, because that depth gives them at least a slight measure of protection. If you notice a ledge, boulder, or even an outsized rock that has a bit of an overhang, some place for a single fish to tuck itself under and still observe the surface overhead, suspect that a trout will be hidden in there. Show your fly to it at least once or twice, and you're highly likely to get it ambushed. Shade is perhaps the best defining factor in reading edge lies. The barest bit of it is often enough to conceal a trout. Always fish it. It doesn't need to be the obvious shade of an overhanging bush or branch; it can just as easily be a small patch of darkness on the bottom cast by a submerged boulder. As the sun moves overhead, and the shade migrates along the bottom, trout will move with it . . . you look for that bit of darkness, and make sure your fly floats directly over it.

Flies are a sort of no-brainer when you're fishing low water, along the edges, after trout have moved

Grasshoppers are one of a trout's favorite and most frequent food items when summer draws to a close.

**Left:** Like the naturals they imitate, easy-to-see hopper patterns are often perfect for fooling low-water trout looking for a morsel falling in from above. PHOTOS BY DAVE HUGHES

# Dave Hughes

there to take advantage of terrestrial insects: that's what you want to imitate. Specifically, I recommend you use what Skip and Rick recommend; they're far wiser about flies than I am. I use a black Quik-Site Ant for ants, in size 16; a Black Foam Beetle for beetles, usually in size 12 or 14; Ed Schroeder's Parachute Hopper for grasshoppers, most often in size 8 or 10; an Olive Beadhead Nymph for inchworms, in size 12 to 14. Naturally I tie special imitations for a few terrestrials that are found in abundance on particular waters that I fish: a big gray hopper for a desert stream in eastern Oregon; an amber-bodied and dun-winged termite dressing when those guys are out in autumn; a size 16 bulbous-bodied brown beetle for one that gets blown out of conifer trees on Fall River and sometimes alders along the Deschutes. Rarely, however, do you need to get more specific than a few generic dressings that look at least a little like what's falling to the water along the edges. Trout there are almost always seeing a variety of arrivals and normally accept them all. They don't get selective. You can even use your Royal Wulffs and Stimulators with beneficial results, at times.

Almost always, until a specific dry imitation has proven itself by drawing up more than a few trout, I dangle a generic nymph on about 2 feet of tippet off the hook bend of the dry fly itself. This is insurance against a drubbing. If it's morning, and insects don't have their engines revved yet, the

The perfect rod for fishing bank water will depend on the kind of stream vegetation and the challenges it presents. RICK HAFELE

nymph will take by far the most trout. If it's a cool day in late summer or early fall, the dangled nymph might work all day. If the water is still cool, usually the result of a watershed upstream that's in excellent condition, then the nymph will succeed until some-

time just before or after noon, when the water warms enough for trout to get their own engines revved up. When the dry fly begins to outperform the nymph, then I simply nip off the sunk fly and continue my fishing. Since the best nymphs are generic, I won't list them here; use your favorites; they'll work best for you. Just be sure to use them in small enough sizes that they don't tug the dry fly under. Bead heads don't hurt, because they tend to sink a nymph to just the right depth to fish in shallow water.

And don't forget to set the hook when your dry fly mysteriously disappears. That's a take to the nymph swimming beneath it.

Tackle and tactics for nibbling at the edges can be analogous to what you'd use on a small stream. The Deschutes River itself, as broad and brawling as they get, is often called two small streams, each of them five feet wide, one of them on either side of the river. If you're working your way upstream, nibbling at one of those edges, you're better off armed with the same gear you'd fish on your favorite small stream than you would be carrying what might work better on one of the monstrous riffles or runs of the same river.

When I'm fishing banks, I like to go light, but I also want enough line weight to turn over flies with some size—those big hoppers. So my line will be a 4- or 5-weight. The best length for the rod depends on the shape of the streamside vegetation. If you're in open country, with no hindrance to your backcast, there is no rea-

Not all trout caught nibbling along the edges will be large, but they will all be beautiful. RICK HAFELE

son not to use an 8¹/₂- to 9-foot rod. If the banks are tight with brush, then a 7¹/₂- to 8-foot rod will serve you better. If you're on a Wisconsin limestoner that wends its way through a tunnel of tall wheat- and ryegrass, then you might want a 9-foot rod or longer to loft your backcast up above all that danger. Alternatively, I fished with an educated angler who preferred a 5- to 6-foot rod to burrow through the same circumstances. On most waters, nibbling at the edges is best accomplished with an 8- to 8¹/₂-foot, 4- or 5-weight rod.

Tactics are quite simple. You amble along, keep yourself out of sight of any lie you're about to fish, be careful not to let your footfalls land with thuds. You've already read those prospective lies. You're armed with the right fly or pair of them. Simply cast upstream as you slip along, showing your offering to any trout that might be tucked in there. It's as simple as fishing any small stream. Books have been written about that.

I've written one myself—*Trout from Small Streams: Second Edition*, Stackpole Books, 2014.

# Late-Season Low

F all has always been my favorite fishing time in general and my favorite time for fishing trout rivers in particular. Days offer the pleasant lack of summer's sizzle—and its accompanying forest fires that fill river valleys with purple-stained smoke. Motel rates are down without the summer festivals that bring drunks to stumble in herds like diseased cattle and drive up the cost of rooms. And the rivers are low and clear.

# Skip Morris

CAROL ANN MORRIS

Clear, low rivers are a specialty item I love, offering specific challenges, strategies, and rewards. We'll start with the challenges. The rewards seem obvious to me (one, in fact, being the challenges) but I'll run over them at the end anyway.

## Stealth, Exposure, and Recent Memory

Low water in late summer and fall is small water, relative to the rest of the year, and the trout know it—they *feel* it. As a result, they also feel vulnerable to predation with so little room for escape, which makes them skittish. Low water is shallower and slower and clearer than usual too, so the fish get a better and perhaps longer look at your fly . . . and everything else. You see where this is going, right? Your fly needs to behave properly, which usually means in a generally natural way or specifically like the creature it imitates. Your leader and line must stay well away from the

fish, so longer leaders and tippets may be in order. Your casts must neither pass the line too near the fish nor throw the line on the water with more than a light drop. And you may need to crouch, stay back from the water, or both, or perhaps approach from well downstream or just well away from the fish. Or perhaps make a long downstream presentation of the fly—an ace up the sleeve for nervous trout.

Smaller, slower, clearer water does make trout wary, but that's not the whole story. Low water typically comes late in the season, and by then the trout have been hammered. They've been hooked and netted and pricked by flies and generally harassed for months and, despite their tiny brains, they're left with a strong impression: Specifically—don't get fooled again. You can debate all day about the extent of a trout's memory, but old hands at trout streams will tell you that late-season trout seem a whole lot smarter than they were in the early season, water conditions aside.

*Scan to watch Video:*
## Trout Stream Stealth

## Tackle

Most fly fishers reach for the same rods and reels and lines for low water that they fish in high water, and that's probably fine. But brimming springtime rivers and heavier lines really do make sense. And famished fall rivers and light lines make just as much sense. So a 6-weight line in spring, a 5 in summer, and a 4 in

the fall is a sound strategy. All of that depends in part on the flies you'll be fishing too, of course, and the size of your river. A really big trout stream like the Deschutes in Oregon or the Upper Columbia in Washington always seems right with a 6-weight line to me. Although I have fished a 4 on the Deschutes to rising trout and must admit it felt good and performed admirably (to the displeasure of a few fish sedately feeding at the surface of a huge eddy).

There are lots of variables when it comes to line weight, and your own preferences count high among them. Bottom line: Use what you like, but if you're ever going to go lighter on your river, low water in autumn would be the time.

**Below:** The rod you like—for any kind of fishing—is as personal as the meal you choose from a menu or the spouse you chose to marry. Still, lines lighter than the all-purpose 6-weight offer advantages when rivers are small and slow and very clear and trout are skittish. RICK HAFELE

Casting from the knees so far back from the water may seem wildly overcautious, but the browns and rainbows of this dead-low creek demand it. CAROL ANN MORRIS

Rods? Again, they're largely about personal preference. But a bit softer and perhaps a slower action than average (more flexible through the butt-section and therefore lazier in response) does offer advantages with low flows. Rod length is really subjective; if you like a particular rod, don't let me or anyone else talk you out of it.

You have to bear in mind too that low-water fishing isn't one-dimensional—sure, you may present size 20 Blue-Winged Olive emerger flies to sedately surface-feeding browns, something of the classic fly fisher's daydream for gentle water. But perhaps instead you're skidding gargantuan size 6 dry flies across the water because October Caddis adults are slapping down to excite the trout. Or maybe you're working a nymph or even a streamer on a sinking-tip line. Go too short or too light or just too gutless on your tackle and you may find yourself struggling. Personally, I rarely go below a 5-weight line and rod in low water unless I'm pretty confident that deep nymphs and streamers and huge dry flies aren't in the picture.

Overall, I tend to be a heavy tippet man—I don't like losing a big fish when one comes along. So 3X tippet is my standard for nymph fishing and 4X my standard for dry flies—though with *big* dry flies I often choose 3X. Low water is different—though I prefer heavy tippet, I'm wide open to fine stuff if fall trout tell me they require it. I've used 6X many times, and 7X and 8X seem to wind up on my leaders every year, again, usually in fall. In my experience, 5X will fool most river trout even in low water, and 6X is usually as fine as I need to go—if the trout are refusing my fly on 6X, it's probably something other than the tippet they dislike. Still, wary trout on tiny insects, and clear, slow currents . . . there *is* a place for the finest tippets.

## Know the Midge and the BWO

With the exception of the massive October Caddis (and those occasional and generally unreliable hatches of late mayflies or other caddis), most of the insects my river trout eat in the low flows of fall are tiny, a lot of Blue-Winged Olive (BWO) mayflies and midges. That varies from one river to the next, but these are really the two mainstay insects of Western trout-river fishing in my experience, be it Washington, Idaho, Colorado, or British Columbia.

The BWO and midge are both big winter hatches too, but that's another matter.

My point? Know what hatches to expect when the water is thin—which normally happens in autumn—and come prepared. The water can be low as early as mid- or late summer too, especially on a dry year. In late summer lots of things are still hatching: all sorts of medium-size caddis, a variety of mayflies, smaller stoneflies, and there may be ants and beetles dropping onto the water from the river's edges. So expect more insect options in mid-August than in October. But in fall, bring some extra flies for midge and BWO hatches (and in the West, perhaps for October Caddis).

## Unnatural Lows

Tailwaters, streams that flow from dams, usually reach their smallest flows in the fall, just as undammed streams do. But if there's a reason to tighten down a river's volume—irrigation, a dry year, whatever—the dam-keeper will do it with a simple

On the whole, your leaders and tippets will be longer for low-water flows than for higher ones. If a 9-foot tapered leader is the norm on your favorite trout river, you might do better with a 12-footer in the fall, especially on broad, flat water with really skittish fish. You may need to increase your tippet length in fall as well. I keep going longer and longer on tippets as the trout in my rivers seem to grow ever more cautious, regardless of conditions, so a 3-foot tippet is my standard now for dry flies and floating emergers. But I'm far more likely to go shorter in spring or summer than in fall. If I were ever to move toward 4 feet of tippet, it would be during low water.

# Skip Morris

The Blue-Winged Olive can hatch in any month of the year, but it usually hatches best during the cold months, providing a lot of fall action when other mayflies are quietly waiting for spring or summer. RICK HAFELE

turn of the dial or whatever adjusts the release from the dam. The solution is simple: even if it's a season when the river should be at a normal flow or high, just disregard that, and if it's low—treat it as low. Maybe the point here is that you'd be wise to carry some low-water flies and tippet and leaders in your vest along with low-water strategies in the back of your mind any time you plan to fish a tailwater.

## Rewards

OK, I promised to talk about the rewards of low-water trout fishing, so . . .

First, as I mentioned, many consider the caution of trout after a long season of angler harassment and

the added nervousness of late-season low water a gift—they like a challenge. Keeps things interesting.

Second, getting up, down, and around a river and finding clear space for back casts is easiest in low water.

Third, your odds of finding solitude on the water (what real fly fisher doesn't crave solitude?) take a leap when, after Labor Day, the kids go back to school and their parents' chances of an extended fishing vacation take a dive.

Fourth, you don't have to wait for what seems half the night to hit that calm, sweet evening rise. In fact, you can have dinner after dark at a reasonable hour.

Autumn low water—I'm a fan.

**BARR EMERGER, BLUE-WINGED OLIVE, DRY**

*John Barr*

| | |
|---|---|
| **Hook:** | #16-20 light wire, standard length to 1X long |
| **Thread:** | Gray 8/0 |
| **Tail:** | Brown dry-fly hackle fibers, trimmed to length |
| **Abdomen:** | Olive and brown buoyant dubbing, blended |
| **Wing Case and Legs:** | Blue-dun dry-fly hackle fibers |
| **Thorax:** | Medium-gray buoyant dubbing |

**Notes:** Imitates hatching BWO mayflies and those that fail to hatch. These days the Barr Emerger is a pretty standard fly, in its various forms, for hatches of Blue-Winged Olive and PMD mayflies. Pull the fibers forward for a wing case, bind them at the hook's eye, split the tips to the sides and bind them, and trim the tips to length.

**PALOMINO MIDGE, BROWN**

*Brett Smith*

| | |
|---|---|
| **Hook:** | #18-22 light wire, humped shank (pupa/emerger hook) |
| **Thread:** | Brown 8/0 or finer |
| **Abdomen:** | Brown New Dub, Magic Dub, or Easy Dubbing, melted on the end |
| **Wing Case and Gills:** | White Z-Lon or Antron yarn |
| **Thorax:** | Brown rabbit fur (or buoyant dubbing, if you're sure you want the fly to float) |

**Notes:** Usually treated with floatant and fished in the water's surface, but it can be dangled below a dry fly.

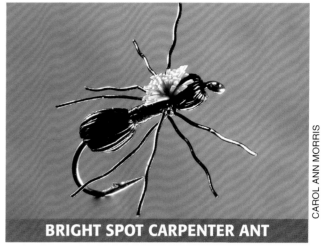

**BRIGHT SPOT CARPENTER ANT**

*Dave Whitlock*

| | |
|---|---|
| **Hook:** | #8-16 light wire, standard length or 1X long |
| **Thread:** | Black 8/0 or 6/0 |
| **Abdomen, Thorax, and Legs:** | Black elk or moose-body hair |
| **Strike Indicator:** | A small bunch of pink or orange deer hair, trimmed short |

**MIKULAK SEDGE**

*Art Mikulak*

| | |
|---|---|
| **Hook:** | #6-10 standard to heavy wire, 1X to 3X long |
| **Thread:** | 6/0 or 3/0 in the body's color |
| **Tail:** | Elk hair (the tail is really part of the wing) |
| **Body and Wing:** | Sections of buoyant dubbing between bunches of elk hair |
| **Hackle:** | One (usually brown), between the last wing section and the head |
| **Head:** | The butts of the final wing section of elk trimmed to a blunt head |

**Notes:** You can tie the Mikulak Sedge to imitate any substantial caddisfly you want by varying hook size and colors. For the October Caddis I like orange thread, orange dubbing, and a brown hackle.

Dave and I started our trip for Idaho's Lochsa River here, at the Lower Columbia River near Portland, Oregon. Interestingly, the water from the Lochsa River also ends up here and travels another 100 miles before finally reaching the Pacific Ocean. RICK HAFELE

*Rick Hafele*

# The Rise and Fall of Fall Fishing

One thing I like about fly fishing is that unexpected situations are to be expected. A trip I took this past fall proved once again how common the unexpected is, and also proved once again the importance of one small mayfly.

Skip playing a fish on a beautiful fall day on the Lochsa. RICK HAFLE

The trip was with Dave Hughes, fellow coauthor and general instigator. We headed for the Lochsa River in Idaho the third week of September. We picked that particular time to coincide with the hatch activity of the October Caddis. October Caddis, also called Fall Caddis, is one of the marquee hatches of the year on many Western streams. It rises to the top of many anglers' must-fish hatches because the insect is large—almost the size of a big stonefly—and it hatches in the fall sometime between mid-September and early November when few other insect hatches are on the water. Because of its size and abundance, some of the biggest fish in the river will forget themselves and willingly take big dry flies off the surface. At least that's what Dave and I hoped for when we got in the car and headed east from Portland.

Planning a fishing trip for most of us is a combination of convenience (when we can find the time to go), purpose (plan to be there at the peak of a hatch), and hope (hope the weather cooperates and doesn't put the hatch and the fishing off). In our

case the timing seemed just right to hit the big October Caddis hatch on the Lochsa. Four years earlier I fished the Lochsa at the same time of year with Skip Morris, his wife Carol, and Peter, a friend of Skip and Carol's from British Columbia, and we had a great week of mild weather and fast fishing. October Caddis adults took to the air and water every afternoon, and the native westslope cutthroat of the Lochsa couldn't have been happier to intercept them. A couple mayflies also made their appearance, usually in the late afternoon and evening, which added another surge of surface activity. All in all, we had a blast, and Dave and I were hoping for a repeat performance.

You probably already know where I'm headed with this story: Things didn't work out quite as we had hoped. It must have been that butterfly in Peru taking off that threw the weather into a tizzy, since the week before we left a typhoon somewhere in the Pacific Ocean sent a wave of rain into the Pacific Northwest and inland as far as Idaho. The storm was followed by unusually cold air, so by the time we left, the normal sunny mild September weather was no longer normal.

The drive from Portland took us up the Columbia River gorge into eastern Washington, following much of the same route that Lewis and Clark did more than two hundred years ago. As an angler I often fantasize about the fly fishing I would have had if I could have been fishing these waters when Lewis and Clark passed by them. Besides the 15 million salmon and steelhead that went up the Columbia each year, the tributaries would have had bountiful populations of native rainbows, cutthroat, and bull trout. Much has changed in two hundred years. In some ways it's a marvel that chinook salmon still manage to find their way back to the Lochsa River to spawn, though their numbers now are but a trickle of their past abundance.

Just before reaching the point where the Snake River joins the Columbia, we turned right and headed almost due east to Lewiston, Idaho. At Lewiston the Clearwater River enters the Snake. The Snake, the Clearwater, the Salmon: These are all major rivers in their own right, and yet they are just a few of the rivers that make the Columbia the largest stream draining into the Pacific Ocean in North America. We followed the Clearwater upstream and watched steel-headers Spey-cast flies into its cold, clear currents with more hope and more patience than I can muster. The road passed through little towns with names like Kamiah and Kooskia that reminded me that Europeans weren't the first settlers along these rivers. Finally we reached the juncture of the Lochsa and Selway rivers, which join to become the Middle Fork of the Clearwater. We turned left up the Lochsa. Daylight had long passed to darkness when we finally

October Caddis larvae feeding on the surface of a boulder.

**Top Right:** The partially removed case shows this October Caddis pupa developing inside its larval case. **Bottom Right:** Once mature, the pupae have to crawl to shore, hopefully before a trout can find them. PHOTOS BY RICK HAFELE

# Rick Hafele

*Scan to watch Video:*
## October Caddis

pulled into the Lochsa Lodge and retrieved the key to our cabin.

We came this far for one main reason: to fish the October Caddis hatch. October Caddis belong to the caddis family Limnephilidae and genus *Dicosmoecus*. Five different species of *Dicosmoecus* live in Western streams with two, *D. gilvipes* and *D. atripes*, the most common and abundant. Except for minor differences in male and female genitalia there's little difference between the five species, so there's no need to worry which species lives in the streams you fish. Mature larvae are easily recognized by their 2-inch-long stony cases. In May and June you can find large numbers of them crawling along the tops of boulders scraping off algae and diatoms for food. Around mid-

July or early August, the larvae stop feeding and look for safe places under boulders and cobble to secure their cases and begin a two-month pupation period sealed up inside. It's during this time that the larvae molt into pupae and the pupae mature. If you pick up a softball-size cobble from a moderate riffle during August and September, it's quite likely you'll see two or three or more large stone cases tightly stuck to the cobble's underside. Then if you carefully peel back the stone case, you'll find a pupa inside. A mature one will have very dark, almost black, wing pads folded back along a tan thorax and creamy-yellow abdomen. If you place it in some water, you can watch it wiggle along. Now imagine how a trout might react to such a morsel moving in the water.

October Caddis adults are one of the largest aquatic insects to emerge in the fall, when abundant trout sometimes throw caution to the wind.

**Left:** Empty October Caddis pupa shucks left behind on a boulder after the adults emerged. PHOTOS BY RICK HAFELE

A cold, overcast day cast its shadow on the October Caddis hatch. Moral of the story: Don't expect to find what you expected. RICK HAFELE

To avoid trout as much as possible, these big caddis emerge at night. The pupae first cut their way out of their stone cases and then crawl and swim along the stream bottom until they reach a shoreline stone upon which they crawl up and out of the water. It's only then that the adults slip out of their pupal skin and fly up to the safety of the streamside trees and shrubs. This is quite different than the daytime, surface film emergence of most other caddis and requires fishing pupa patterns deep along the stream bottom, usually early in the morning. Trout that fed during the night on pupae are still happy to take more in the early morning light.

After mating on nearby trees or shrubs, the females fly back to the water throughout the afternoon and evening to lay their eggs. The awkward flying adults dip to the water's surface, providing a great opportunity for trout to take them. To match them, a large dry fly fished either dead-drift or twitched on the surface makes for a great day of fishing.

Dave and I woke up to a dark, cold sky the next morning and quickly decided to throw another log in the little woodstove that heated our cabin and take our time eating breakfast. October Caddis adults wouldn't be flying around until the air warmed up to at least above freezing. We also knew that such cold weather could mean that no adults would fly all day, which was pretty much what we found once we got on the water just before noon. Four years ago adults flitted and hopped over the riffles and runs all afternoon. This day we saw only a few adults, and they weren't over the water. In fact it was a day when the river kept its secrets well hidden, and the surface flowed quietly without the disturbing movement of insects or fish. This meant that to catch some fish we'd need to use nymphs. If you've read any of my other books or articles, you probably know I'm not opposed to fishing nymphs, and in fact quite enjoy it. But fishing nymphs all day somehow didn't match the vision of rising cutthroat trout I had in mind when I left Portland.

Westslope cutthroat are native to the Lochsa River, but they may not have been the first trout in the river. The evolutionary history of trout distribution

# Rick Hafele

throughout the West is complex and fascinating. For decades, fish biologists have been sorting it out. Even what to call a species has been a moving target, resulting in many changes in the taxonomy of western trout species. Currently westslope cutthroat are classified as *Oncorhynchus clarki lewisi*, which, depending on what author you read, is just one of 9 to 14 recognized subspecies of cutthroat. Except for coastal cutthroat, cutthroat trout evolved isolated above barrier falls on the large Western rivers, falls like Shoshone Falls on the Snake River, or trapped in inland seas and large lakes without any connection to other trout species. Such isolation over thousands of years resulted in the variety of subspecies we see today.

Some theories suggest that before rainbow trout found their way into the Clearwater River, Yellowstone cutthroat (*Oncorhynchus clarki bouvieri*) were the first trout in the Clearwater drainage, including the Lochsa. When rainbows arrived in the Columbia and Snake Rivers, Yellowstone cutthroat couldn't compete and were eliminated. Then westslope cutthroat, most likely from populations in the Clark Fork River drainage, found their way into the Clearwater system and have been able to coexist with rainbows. This of course all took place thirty thousand to fifteen thousand years ago. However they arrived, westslope cutthroat are now ancient survivors in many Rocky Mountain streams.

Anglers often consider cutthroat species to be easy marks when it comes to fooling them with flies. It's also often assumed that trout are less selective when feeding on nymphs than dry flies. Such generalizations, however, never make for solid footing when it comes to Mother nature, and especially trout. I have found cutthroat to be capable of very selective feeding behavior on both drys and nymphs. Remembering the success I had fishing dry flies several years ago, I couldn't help myself and tied on a size 10 Stimulator. After a couple half-hearted tries and one little fish, it became apparent that dry flies weren't the answer. It was time to nymph.

I almost always use two nymphs, and the first one I tied on was a pupa pattern called the Brick Back October Caddis pupa, developed by Skip Morris. This pupa matches the size, shape, and color of the natural beautifully and is heavily weighted so it will fish close to the stream bottom where the naturals move

**Below:** A beautiful westslope cutthroat, *Oncorhynchus clarki lewisi.* RICK HAFELE

Cutthroat trout are ancient enough to have reached most stream systems before waterfalls like this blocked their passage. Once the waterfalls formed, they isolated the cutthroat from any other trout. RICK HAFELE

on their shoreward journey. Though we weren't seeing many adults, I couldn't help but think that enough were emerging. For the second fly I tied on a small (size 16) dark mayfly nymph. I routinely find that small nymphs out-fish large ones and small mayflies are a common food in stream drift.

The results weren't spectacular. Yes, I caught some trout—and whitefish—on the nymphs, with nearly all taking the small mayfly nymph, but the fishing was anything but red hot. The day continued to stay cold and dark, the kind of day when you expect it to start snowing any moment.

The next morning was even colder, well below freezing, but the sun was out. I'm always amazed at the instant warmth a few sun rays can provide . . . by late morning it was possible to cast without ice forming in the guides, something I much prefer. We spent some time exploring. The Lochsa is followed closely by a two-lane highway from its mouth to headwaters. If you keep driving east you end up in Montana,

along the Bitterroot River. The highway provides dozens of pullouts along the Lochsa where you can access the river.

A little after one o'clock we stopped at a pullout and peered down at a smooth run below a tumbling riffle, and to our surprise we saw rising trout. All we could see flying above the water were tiny insects, so we assumed a midge hatch had stimulated the trout's interest. It took a little time to rig up for fishing small dry flies, but things still looked good when we got down to the river. It also became clear that the bugs weren't midges, but tiny Blue-Winged Olive (BWO) mayflies.

Blue-Winged Olives are probably the most important mayfly in trout streams across North America. They are also a confusing group because the common name, Blue-Winged Olive, actually applies to ten or even twenty different species. They all fall into the family Baetidae and most belong to the genus *Baetis*, but species of *Acentrella, Diphetor, Procloeon,* and

Dave playing a nymph-caught trout.

**Right:** This size 22 Blue-Winged Olive provided the only real surface-feeding activity of our trip.

PHOTOS BY RICK HAFELE

more, also fall into the BWO camp. No matter what their Latin name might be, Blue-Winged Olives are widespread and abundant. They emerge multiple times throughout the year and consistently create excellent surface fishing. They are also small, and sometimes really tiny. The BWOs on the Lochsa were tiny, like size 22s. I don't carry a lot of 22s, but I did find a sparsely tied size 20 BWO dun pattern. After tying on three or four feet of 6X tippet, I felt ready to catch some trout.

The smooth currents made getting a drag-free drift a bit of a challenge. The high bank also made it diffi-cult to get a long enough cast to reach the rising fish without putting your fly into the trees covering the

bank. I walked downstream, picking on fish that were rising only 10 or 15 feet out from the bank by casting downstream with a parachute cast. It worked, but I put down a number of fish in the process. As I looked upstream, Dave was changing patterns—again. (I later learned he had left a couple flies in tree branches, but I swore I wouldn't tell anyone.) We fished this run for a couple hours. We didn't catch as many fish as it seemed we should have, but there were trout, and they were rising, and they were difficult to catch. The afternoon slipped by like magic.

What I find amazing about BWOs is how such a small insect can generate so much interest from trout. I don't know why, maybe they taste really good, but for some reason whenever BWOs are available—which is often—trout like to take them. I had an experience a couple weeks later that drove this home even more. I was fishing a trout stream in southern British Columbia with a good friend from Vancouver, specifically to fish a hatch of mayflies of the genus *Cinygmula* (family Heptageniidae), commonly known as the Dark Red Quills. And we found them. Every afternoon about 2:00, the little reddish tan duns with pale yellow wings, about a size 16, started hatching. The trout, wild rainbows in this case, took them with leisurely sips—with one exception. On the third day, the Dark Red Quills started emerging right on time, but much to our frustration the trout completely ignored them. Then about 3:00, tiny, size 20 BWO duns also started popping up on the surface. Immediately the trout started rising to the BWOs. I couldn't believe it, but the trout ignored for an hour the readily available *Cinygmula* duns and then went after the little BWOs as soon as they hit the surface. Don't ask

me why! We had to fish little size 20 dun patterns to catch any fish.

Dave and I caught a few of the little BWO duns and put them in small containers in our cooler. The next morning we set up our cameras with macro lenses and took photos of the duns. It's eye-opening to look at these insects up close. They seem way too small and delicate to survive, but they not only survive, they thrive and have done so for literally millions of years.

Two other mayflies also showed up during our stay on the Lochsa. One produced some interesting fishing with wet flies and some of the best fish of the trip. This mayfly was a Mahogany Dun (family Leptophlebiidae, genus *Paraleptophlebia*), a common mayfly hatch in the fall and spring on many trout streams throughout North America. Mahogany Duns can be easily recognized by their mahogany color, medium size (usually about a size 14), and three tails on nymphs, duns, and spinners. Mature nymphs

A *Paraleptophlebia* dun on the left and an *Ameletus* dun on the right. They look somewhat alike, but you can tell them apart from the number of tails—3 versus 2.

**Right:** Trout sometimes couldn't decide whether they should take this *Cinygmula* dun, but they always took BWOs when they were available.

PHOTOS BY RICK HAFELE

Fishing small size 20 and 22 dry flies in the smooth water below riffles proved the best way to catch the Lochsa's beautiful cutthroat when BWOs appeared. PHOTOS BY RICK HAFELE

hang out in relatively shallow (a foot or less) water near shore. When ready to emerge, the nymphs swim to the surface or crawl out of the water onto nearby exposed rocks, so the duns hatch on dry land. But some of the nymphs apparently get washed into the current and some of the duns get blown into the water because when Mahogany Duns are around, fishing a simple soft-hackle wet fly often works well, even when there's no obvious trout feeding.

The last mayfly that showed up I initially thought was a close relative of the March Brown—a clinger mayfly of the family Heptageniidae. However, after looking at some I collected under the microscope, they turned out to be a species of the genus *Ameletus* (family Ameletidae) commonly called Brown Duns. There are many species of this genus (roughly thirty-four in North America), with some emerging in the spring and others in the fall. Like the Mahogany Duns, the nymphs prefer to crawl out above the

---

**Below:** The rainbows in this British Columbia stream shunned one mayfly on the surface only to readily take BWOs when they started emerging. RICK HAFELE

water on streamside rocks for dun emergence. We rarely saw duns of either the *Paraleptophlebia* or *Ameletus* on the water, but we collected them by walking along the shoreline looking on the boulders and cobbles right next to the water. Neither mayfly produced the surface action of the Blue-Winged Olives, but their presence did seem to create some opportunities to catch fish swinging wet flies, which added another interesting twist to our trip.

Which reminds me, we did take this trip to fish the October Caddis hatch. Well, the October Caddis must have waited until October to hatch, because they never did show up in abundance during this late-September trip. As we drove back down the Lochsa toward its confluence with the Selway and the beginning of the Clearwater, I could imagine October Caddis pupae sealed up in their cases anxious to emerge and the big adults fluttering over the water. Every fishing trip is a trip into the unknown, which I suppose is a big reason they are so much fun. Just make sure you have some small Blue-Winged Olive patterns with you when you leave.

# October Caddis Patterns

Skip Morris

## For the Larva

Oswald's BH Rock Roller stirred up considerable excitement when it first appeared a few years ago. Why not? It's a clever design. It uses various colors of rubber strand bound around a hook's shank, compressed together and trimmed almost as deer hair is flared and cut to make a bass bug. The colors of the strands create the look of the variously colored grains of sand and tiny fragments of stone that make up the October Caddis's case. It's a fun and challenging fly at the vise and a solid trout catcher.

**OSWALD'S BH ROCK ROLLER**

*Duncan Oswald*

| Hook: | #6-16 heavy wire, 3X long |
|---|---|
| Head: | Black metal bead |
| Weight: | Lead or lead-substitute wire |
| Thread: | Black, heavy |
| Abdomen: | Black, brown, tan, and white round rubber strand mixed with gold and silver High Voltage Mylar strand |
| Thorax: | Black rabbit blended with a little black Antron |

**Notes:** Duncan prefers a hook with a kinked shank. For the abdomen, pick up a long hank of the rubber strand and Mylar, and bind the ends at the hook's bend. Trim off the hank, leaving the cut ends. Draw back the ends of the rubber strand and Mylar and bind on the hank in front, cut the front end of the hank again, and continue this way up most of the shank. Whip-finish and trim the thread after the abdomen's built, and then trim the rubber strand and Mylar to make the larva's case.

## For the Pupa

You may have seen my Brick Back October Caddis, an imitation of the pupa, in our companion book, *Tactics for Trout*—but there's always another good fly (if not another dozen or even a hundred) for the job, whatever that job is. So here's a pupa pattern that proved itself to me clear back in the early 1990s on Oregon's Lower Deschutes River—prime October Caddis water. I was playing host on a TV show and drifting the river with a local guide. He rigged me up with an October Caddis Nymph trailing (to the best of my recollection) an equally large and heavier nymph of some kind. The flies worked, especially the October Caddis Nymph. By early evening I'd brought perhaps ten or twelve rainbows to the net, and a couple were large. I had lost as many, and the guide and the cameraman were both smiling and joking around—a sign that was always a great relief to me.

At this point, you need to know that while all *artificial* flies that imitate underwater insects are called "nymphs," there is no *real* "caddis nymph." During its life cycle, a caddisfly lives as a larva and a pupa, and

**OCTOBER CADDIS NYMPH**

*Paul Wolflick*

| Hook: | #8 standard to heavy wire, 3X long |
|---|---|
| Thread: | Black 8/0, 6/0, or 3/0 |
| Weight: | Lead or lead-substitute wire |
| Rib: | Pale orange D-Rib, V-Rib, Larva Lace, or the like |
| Abdomen: | Rusty orange rabbit |
| Hackle: | Furnace hen hackle |
| Head: | Peacock herl |

SKIP MORRIS

finally as an adult, but never as a nymph. So don't let the name October Caddis Nymph throw you. OK, now back to that misnamed—but effective—fly pattern.

This nymph, tied in the original style, doesn't rush for the depths the way our current metal-bead nymphs do, which is fine if you're fishing the fly as a trailer off a really heavy fly as I was long ago for the video camera. And sometimes the October Caddis Nymph's layer of lead-substitute wire is just right for putting the fly down right where you want it in shallow or slower currents. But if you want it to hurry down for the riverbed, that's simple: Keep the wire wraps and add a standard or tungsten bead for a head.

It's a straightforward fly but a good one that includes the details that matter most.

## For the Adult

My response a few years ago to discovering that wool is stubbornly buoyant was to develop my Woolly Wing fly pattern. It started out as an imitation of caddis adults—and still is—but it's proved itself for imitating stoneflies of all sorts as well. I won't say that the woolen wing of the pattern just won't let this fly sink—it can grow sodden to the point that everything goes down. But normally, a quick snap at the end of a casting stroke or two leaves a previously waterlogged Woolly Wing again riding on top. I've found few dry caddis imitations that come anywhere close to the Woolly Wing's marathon buoyancy. I wish I could claim it was my brilliant design work that keeps this fly floating so long, but all I did was discover that wool doesn't like to sink and then make a wing out of it. The wing-body-wing sections aren't my idea either; you (and I) can thank Canadian Art Mikulak, creator of the Mikulak Sedge, for that. (I'll take credit for trimming the wing to shape and trading Art's conventional hackle for a parachute hackle, though.)

The Woolly Wing, you should know, doesn't float high. It settles down onto the water and stays there, floating low (and floating long). That's fine, though, because settling down to float low is just what big caddis adults often do.

Other times they scurry, and that's fine too since the Woolly Wing can be made to skim the surface of a river and appear to scurry.

It's an easy fly to find out there, despite its low posture and low profile and darkish coloring, thanks to that bright fuzzy dome that acts like a beacon atop its hackle.

A Canadian friend once asked me if I'd ever tried adding rubber-strand legs to my Woolly Wing. I said I hadn't, but after his comment I did. Thus, the Leggy Woolly Wing. I've seen enough evidence on the water by now to believe that those long swaying legs on big Woolly Wings draw extra strikes.

SKIP MORRIS

## LEGGY WOOLLY WING, ORANGE

*Skip Morris*

| | |
|---|---|
| **Hook:** | #6-10 standard to heavy wire (slow-curve shank is optional) |
| **Thread:** | Orange 6/0 or 3/0 |
| **Body and Wing:** | Sections of tan-brown or brown wool wing and darkish-orange buoyant dubbed body; trim the wool to wing shape |
| **Indicator:** | Yellow egg yarn or wool |
| **Legs:** | Brown flat or round rubber strand, plain, barred, or speckled |
| **Hackle:** | Parachute hackle |

**Notes:** Use a thinner hank of wool for each new section of wing. Four or five sections are about right for a size 8 hook. Trim the wool to the shape of a caddis wing before creating the thorax and parachute hackle and the rest. The wing and body should cover two-thirds of the shank and no more—if the wing is too long, the thorax will slope steeply and want to collapse forward.

Bind the egg yarn at the front of the wing atop the hook with a slim band of tight thread, pull up the ends of the yarn or wool and bind them as a firm base for the hackle. Then bind the stripped stem of the hackle up along that base.

Bind the rubber leg strands on the sides of the shank with a narrow thread collar right behind the parachute wing, dub around the legs and parachute wing base, draw the legs back and secure them in a material clip or with hackle pliers or tape, wind the parachute hackle and bind and trim its tip, and then dub to the hook's eye.

When the weather turned unfriendly during a large portion of our trip, nymphing became the core tactic and took an outsize number of trout for us, though we turned to it only when the trout were not attracted to something on the surface.

DAVE HUGHES

*Dave Hughes*

# Tactics on the Lochsa

The Lochsa River in Idaho is big, beautiful, and brutally boul-dered, probably not the perfect place for a right-handed fel-low still recovering from a broken right collarbone. If I were a quarterback, I'd have been on the injured list. But I'd long ago learned to cast left-handed, and a trip with Rick is always an adven-ture, so I decided to push it a little. As is normal, once we got on the river, I wound up pushing it a lot.

Big boulders on the bottom of the Lochsa River make it difficult to wade, but they also provide lies for nice trout almost everywhere. The clear water sometimes makes it possible to watch a trout rise all the way from the bottom, take a fly, and turn back down with it. DAVE HUGHES

In case you haven't fished it, or driven the gorgeous Route 12 alongside it, I'll describe the Lochsa a bit. Its uppermost tributaries arise on the highest ridges west of the continental divide. Where the river gathers some size and bounds down the Rocky Mountains from Lolo Pass, it's as clear as air, bottomed with big boulders and an absence of gravel, which is too light to seat itself against the fierce strength of the current. I've never fished those upper miles, in the first part because it never looks like a trout would find a place to hold in all that violence, in the second part because it always looks like I'd bust something if I tried to wade it.

Many miles downstream, the river is greatly enlarged, but it levels out a bit and becomes fishable in places, if never easy to wade. It trends to broad and frothed riffles shelving off into long and fairly deep runs, which on occasion slow down and deepen further into giant pools. The water remains clear so

that you can get a position up above it, peer into it, see big trout, and at least as often big whitefish, holding in scattered ones, twos, and sometimes small pods over that massively bouldered bottom.

If you haven't puzzled it out by now, the Lochsa is a river on which you'll need your stout Folstaf and where sturdy and studded brogues are critical. If you decide to attempt it with non-felt soles that lack studs, get in some practice on the backstroke before departing for the trip. We fished it in late September. Air temperatures in afternoon got into the low 60s F, but water temperatures were in the mid 40s. We gave no thought to wading wet.

Our approaches were quite a contrast. Rick, who had fished the river on an earlier fall trip with Skip Morris, knew enough to leave the car with two graphite rods rigged: one for nymphs, the other for dry flies. I, who had only nibbled at the edges of the Lochsa once, long in the past on the way from Oregon to Montana, carried only one rod. Because I was at work on a major project involving wet-fly fishing, that rod was an old favorite bamboo, a 7¹/₂-foot Leonard Duracane, which is perfect for wets, fine for drys, but marginal at best for nymph fishing, which I generally avoid doing with bamboo rods.

The first day was cold. Rick, going on memory of what had worked on his last trip with Skip, started with an October Caddis dry fly. It was early in the hatch, and naturals were scant. I saw just two or three all day, not the sorts of concentrations that would draw trout into holding positions high in the water. When one of the big, lumbering beasts lowered itself over the water to deposit its eggs, a trout showed interest and rushed up to take a swat at it, but missed. Rick tried a dry imitation that had fewer

---

**Below:** When wet-fly fishing, especially upstream, it's helpful to loft the rod and establish an even curve in the line between the rod tip and point where the line enters the water. Any change in this curve is an indication that a trout is fiddling with your fly out there, and it's time to do something about it. DAVE HUGHES

evasive maneuvers, and a very small number of trout managed to nail it. He started in the broad but even flows of a run, about 4 to 6 feet deep. His casts were upstream, usually along current seams, or over submerged boulders that sent slight boils up toward the surface. But it was not necessary to cover specific lies with the big size 10 flies. On that sort of bouldered bottom, the current is broken everywhere, and trout can hold anywhere.

Rick's few trout were beautiful when he held them in his hands: cutthroats, bronze-sided, heavily spotted, crimson slashed, with almost transparent orange fins. One was over 16 inches long. They were, however, sparse compared to his trip with Skip, when the weather was much warmer and a lot more of the big caddis were in the air and on the water.

While Rick tested his dry flies lower down the run, I slipped in at the head of it, right where an exuberant riffle dropped in, and began working it with a slight modification of famous Davy Wotton's wet-fly method. I studied Davy's DVDs *Wet Fly Ways* and *Wet Fly Tying*, and when I got a chance, I fished with him on his home White River in Arkansas. Boiled down to

# Dave Hughes

an oversimplification, his rig calls for three wet flies, a supple floating line, and a 10- to 12-foot rod. His method, again overly condensed, calls for a cast either slightly upstream, straight across, or slightly downstream, with the rod held high and the flies kept in close contact as they're teased through their swing. The key that I learned from Davy—among many other things (the day was an education)—is in the slight arc that the line makes as it descends from the lofted rod tip to the point where it enters the water. This curve serves as your indicator, both of the way the flies are working in the water while you fish them, and of any

activity a trout might cause when it takes one of them. If that curve stops, hesitates, or begins to straighten out, you've got a trout interviewing your fly, and you need to do something about it.

My interpretation of Davy Wotton's long-rod, three-fly method shortened the rod to my little bamboo, and reduced the count of flies to two. I experimented with what I've come to call an "anchor wet," a sparse wet fly, usually a winged Hare's Ear, tied on a heavy size 6 or 8 curved-shank nymph hook. My main purpose for the fly is to achieve as much depth as possible while staying within wet-fly traditions—

The author's favorite "anchor wet," a sparse Hare's Ear tied on a heavy nymph hook. Its purpose, in theory, is to sink fast and deep and to provide something to brace one or two dropper flies against, but it winds up catching an outsize number of trout when used as part of such a rig.

**Right:** The author's rough version of Davy Wotton's exceptional Muddler Daddy. It's not clear if this is a wet fly or streamer, but it's usually fished as the top dropper in a two- or three-fly rig, and as such it is fished most often as a damp fly, either just beneath the surface or dangled in and out of it. When trout rise to take it in a river with clear water, such as the Lochsa, it's often possible to watch it all happen. Though the Muddler Daddy is most often associated with craneflies—daddy longlegs—it's not out of reason to suspect that trout might mistake it for a drowned Fall Caddis adult. PHOTOS BY DAVE HUGHES

using no weight on the shank. But I suppose I've stepped out of bounds with that far-from-traditional hook style. This anchor wet I tied on the point.

The top fly, or dropper, was the same one Davy rigged for me on the White River, his Muddler Daddy. I fished it for the first time with him. It has since become a favorite in the only way that flies achieve that position: It has caught a lot of trout for me. In his DVD, Davy calls the Muddler Daddy fly his anchor, because it pushes lots of water, but I worked on a shrimp boat in my youth, and use the term "anchor" to mean something heavy that achieves instant depth.

I waded in at the head of the run, made my initial casts into the riffle upstream from it, gave the two flies a few feet of free drift to sink. When they swung into position slightly downstream from me, I lifted the rod tip, got that curve installed that Davy Wotton recommends, and followed the two flies through their drift and swing. It was necessary at times to mend the line, in order to slow the flies. At other times I fed line into the drift, flicking it onto the water with slight upstream rolls before lifting the rod tip and regaining the stoop of the line between rod tip and where the line entered the water.

My fishing, like Rick's, was less than brisk, but at the same time highly satisfying. Often enough, the curve of the line would make some slight attempt at straightening out. Almost always, when I tightened up on it, a trout would be out there, hanging onto the anchor wet, and it would be angered by the sudden stinging of the hook.

With the anchor wet to seat it firmly in the current, I was able to draw the dropper fly, the big Muddler Daddy, to a point just beneath the surface, and sometimes even up high enough to dance it in and out of the surface. Most trout took the deeper anchor wet, invisibly, and were detected by the change in the curve of that line. But a few lifted off the bottom, approached the upper fly slowly, sipped it, turned back down with it. I was able to see the entire approach, take, and turn in water that was so clear. I could almost see the startled expression on a trout's frontal physiognomy when I pulled it up short by setting the hook.

Rick and I were enjoying slow fishing, in our almost exactly opposite ways, when in mid-afternoon we began to see a few rises out on the open water of a long, flat run. At first we were unable to see what

prompted the trout to feed on the surface. Rick spotted the insects in the air before we were able to see them on the water. They were mayfly duns, flying low in the cool autumn air, escaping the water and winging it about head high toward riverside vegetation. Rick captured one in his hat, and it quickly became evident why we weren't seeing them on the water, out where the trout were getting a bit busier feeding on them. They were Blue-Winged Olives, about size 20 or 22. We had not expected them. But they're so common, everywhere we fish, that we rarely go unprepared for them.

At least Rick was ready. He sat on a rock, added a tippet of 6X, tied on a floating imitation he's worked out over many BWO hatches—not much more than a ball of CDC fluff on such a small hook. It didn't take him long to get into trout, and his success became, I'm forced to confess, a spur to my own frustration. There is little like sitting on your own rock, some ways away, fumbling with your rigging and watching a guy who is into trout and shouting, albeit quietly, about it.

I don't know that I've ever had a hatch in which so many problems got all gathered together. First I nipped off my two wet flies, which left me a 3X leader that was quite long, because that's the way I fish a two-fly wet rig. I tugged at the tip of a 4X tippet spool and about 6 inches came away, and that was the end of my 4X. I'd been fishing all of the previous season with it, and suddenly the spool was empty. Then I turned to the 5X and remembered I'd loaned it to my wife when she ran out not long earlier, and I'd planned to replace it but forgot to in the excitement of breaking my shoulder. So I was down to 6X. I had a mild excuse for all this; my broken collarbone had cost me all of spring and most of summer fishing, and all my trips since had been taken to tiny waters, using my small-stream belt bag, which held full spools of 4X and 5X, but which was also about 500 miles behind me at home.

I spooled off 3 feet of 6X, somehow lost my grip on it, and a soft wind blew it either up into bankside ferns or somewhere out onto the pool. I never did see where it went, though I thrashed around in both the vegetables and the water hoping I'd reconnect with it. Finally I extracted another 3 feet of 6X, but by this time had lost the end of my leader, which had fallen back inside the guides, and I had to restring it. I got the 6X fixed to the 3X end of it with a lumpy

Long runs with riffles at their heads and sometimes pools farther down are typical of the Lochsa. It's big water, best fished with long rods and a variety of tactics, depending on what trout might be doing at any given moment.
DAVE HUGHES

surgeon's knot, which surprisingly held, and tied on a size 20 Sparkle Dun, one of a row of half a dozen of them in my BWO box, all tied so long in the past that the hooks were a bit rusty. I didn't think much about that, was happy to finally launch myself, wade into

position upstream and a bit across from a little line of rising trout.

I made my first cast, a cross-stream reach, fed some slack into the drift, and all was perfect as it should be. The first trout in the lineup rose, took the

when your partner downstream is still busy landing and releasing trout after trout.

After the third "refusal rise" I decided I needed to change to another pattern. I brought the fly in, looked at it, and discovered it was broken off at the bend. You've all read about that next great progression we're all going to make when fishing over hatches: We'll use flies tied on hooks with no points, so that we get the satisfaction of the take without inflicting any agony on the trout . . . Well, I wasn't quite ready to go there that day.

I tied on another of the flies from that short row of them in the box, cast it out, had the pleasure of another rise, missed the strike. I was onto the problem enough by then to bring the fly in and check the hook point, which as you already know was missing. I snipped it off in disgust, tied on a fly from an entirely different row of them, dressed it with floatant, turned to look for a trout over which to cast it, and discovered that the hatch had ended. There were no more rises.

The BWO emergence turned out to be short, less than an hour, which I had completely wasted. When I got back to the little lodge fly shop, I rushed in to buy some 4X and 5X tippet, but they had not replenished their tippet stock as the season got on and had nothing left but 7X.

If there is a lesson in this, I doubt I need to point it out: Check your tippet spools, hooks, and everything else before you depart on a trip to a river that doesn't have fly shops sprinkled all up and down it.

The next day the temperature dropped from cool to cold, and fishing the surface didn't seem quite so sensible. Rick rigged at once in the way for which he's most famous—he's author of *Nymph Fishing Rivers and Streams*—with the standard strike indicator and split shot rig. He fished the bottom of the same sorts of runs he'd fished the day before on the surface. His production went up, and in truth is the most efficient way to fish such difficult water, at least on days when trout are not so happy to rush up to the surface.

I watched Rick a while, at his usual task of hooking, landing, and releasing more trout than I do. Then I decided to try fishing wet flies at the same level he fished his nymphs: right above the bottom. I moved up to the head of a short pool, right where a riffle plunged over a ledge and entered deeper water in a rush. I rigged with a heavy anchor wet and a

fly, tipped down with it. I raised the rod to seat the hook. It came away with a tiny *tick*, which can happen in the normal course of casting over rising trout, so I cast again. It took a few more tries before the placement and drift of the fly became perfect once more, and another trout rose. I set the hook again, and it came away again. That is not entirely unusual, though such misses can become a bit bothersome

# Dave Hughes

Rick with a pretty, though not large, Lochsa River cutt, this one taken on a soft-hackled wet fly fished on the swing in a long and gentle run. DAVE HUGHES

smaller soft-hackle, figuring the one would take me deep and the other might entice trout into taking. Rather than casting across stream, or even across and down, for the traditional wet-fly swing, I cast almost straight up into the froth of the riffle and then mended and tended line in any way that I could, allowing the force of the down-diving currents to deliver my flies as deep as they would into the pool. When the flies came abreast of me I turned and followed them, at the same time lifting my rod to get as nearly as possible into touch with them without raising them out of their depths.

Only in the lower portion of the drift, and on into the ultimate lift, was I able to have any chance to detect takes, because the line was too slack in the upper, sinking part of the drift. And I did get takes. Again, they were usually telegraphed to me in the form of some slight change in the curve of the line

between my rod tip and the water. Some of the fish I caught were cutthroats, a few of them of very nice size. But most were whitefish because it turns out that every pool on the Lochsa has a gathering of these down near the bottom. I didn't complain; they're big, strong, and as difficult to fool as any trout. They put up a fine fight, and since I'm not planning to eat any of them anyway, it's not a demeaning thing to me if the fish I catch while trout fishing are not exactly trout.

It was a bit of an adventure, learning to catch both those trout and whitefish on deeply sunk wet flies. The largest conclusion I came to, however, was that I must be hooking only about one in ten, or at best one in five, of the fish that took my fly. In truth, the standard indicator-and-shot rig, employed by Rick still in sight downstream, so often with his rod bent, was much more effective.

That second afternoon we were more watchful for rises, which to those size 22 BWOs were somewhat subtle. We also positioned ourselves on a long run that bordered on being a slow pool so that when the rise started we'd be on the sort of water we'd fished the day before. The hatch began to trickle off at around the same time, in the neighborhood of 2:30, and we rigged instantly for it, Rick by simply laying down his nymph rod and picking up his dry-fly rod, me by again nipping off my wet flies, adding 3 feet of 6X, and going right to flies with no rust on their hooks.

Though the trout were cutthroats, which are in theory stupid, and the water far up there in Idaho was wild, it would be beneficial to point out that the fly needed to be a fairly accurate representation of the natural, and the presentation needed to show that fly to the trout in a natural manner, before they'd have anything to do with it. Rick stuck with his CDC pattern, and I used a size 22 Sparkle Dun. But somewhere during the short hatch, I experimented with a parachute pattern with an orange wing, in hopes trout would be willing to take it and I'd have an easier time seeing it. Trout had no interest in it.

I also isolated a small pod of trout and tried them with upstream casts. Though I was able to place the fly perfectly, and get what I considered good drifts time after time, I was not able to entice a trout into taking the fly until I presented it on either cross-stream reach casts or downstream wiggle casts. Those selective trout were insistent that the fly come to them ahead of the warning line and leader and without even the slightest hint of drag.

When all was right, and the fly was placed within a foot or so of the trout's feeding lane, then the results were somewhat predictable, though of course far from certain. Still, we were both able to sting a sufficient number of trout before the hatch ended after only an hour or so. Then it seemed about the right time to head back to the lodge.

The last afternoon of the trip we suffered through rain that was moderate and steady. It was cold and somewhat miserable, but we were pretty well prepared for it with slickers and rainproof packs, which are necessities on the Lochsa in fall. We declared it a perfect day for the BWO hatch and expected it to go on for much more than an hour. We positioned ourselves, as we had each day before, on the sort of long, smooth run where the BWOs had come off the previous two days and the trout had consistently risen to take them. We waited and waited. Nothing happened. We pulled up stakes, rushed upstream and down, looking for them elsewhere. Nothing ever happened anywhere.

We drove back to a favorite riffle that entered a pool and then leveled out into a long run of even current speed and depth. We'd had luck there before and decided it would be a good place to end the trip. For some reason I got it into my head that I wanted to catch some of those big fish down in the depths of the pool that sometimes arrived at hand as cutthroats, other times as whitefish. I didn't care which, but I wanted to end with some easy action, so I strung a long graphite rod, rigged with a big strike indicator, a brace of weighted nymphs, and a couple of split shot on the tippet. It turned out to be effective enough. I caught the bottom on the first cast.

I lost everything and patiently re-rigged it all. I cast again, caught a nice trout, landed it, released it, cast once more and hooked the bottom again. After another long session of totally re-rigging, in light that was beginning to fail, I caught a couple of nice trout, one a cutt and the other not. Then I hung the bottom again, broke everything off, reeled up and quit.

Only then did I turn my attention to Rick, downstream in the run, fishing it placidly by casting a soft-hackled wet fly far out across it, letting it swing down and around on the gentle currents of the long run, mending when needed to slow it. He only hooked half a dozen trout, and only a few of them were 16 inches long. He never did get near enough to the bottom to hang up, and therefore spent all of his time fishing, none re-rigging.

I ended the trip with wading staff elbow, a sore knee, and a collarbone that felt like it had been snapped again. But those few fall days on that gorgeous river, catching beautiful trout and somewhat short of ugly whitefish when I wasn't hung up on the bottom, made it all worth it . . . I think.

*Skip Morris*

# The Off-Season Headliner

A parade of all sorts of mayflies rules the standard trout-river season of late spring into early fall, but no mayfly causes more excited chatter among fly fishers during the long off-season than *Baetis* (properly pronounced "bee'tus," according to my entomologist coauthor Rick Hafele). *Baetis* hatches all over North America, in Washington State's Yakima River, Colorado's South Platte, Alberta's Bow, Michigan's Au Sable, New York's Beaverkill—and the list goes on and on. This mayfly covers ground.

# Skip Morris

There are other off-season mayflies that can put on a good show. The Eastern Gordon Quill can bring trout up for anglers waiting on April snowbanks, and the Western March Brown mayfly makes for good late-winter action on some Western rivers and can return for a lively second round in fall. But compared with *Baetis*, the appearances of these and the few other cold-season mayfly competitors seem disappointingly brief—*Baetis* just keeps coming back, whether as a thin scattering of duns or as a riot covering all the decent water on a river in October or November, or perhaps February or March.

But other mayflies needn't compete with *Baetis*; instead, they can team up with it. I fished with my wife, Carol, once on Colorado's South Platte River when one mayfly passed off to another mayfly the duty of holding the trout up feeding at the surface for

hours. It was an October day with clouds scooting intermittently across the sun, a cool day of unsteady wind. I stood atop a big, pale boulder reaching my casts around an enormous rock to the few trout that held and sipped at the occasional *Baetis* duns riding into the pool on a wrinkled ribbon of current. The water bounded straight in; settled just enough to please one or two trout; glanced off a big, isolated boulder about halfway through; and then continued at a new angle lightly down through the quiet remainder of the clear, dark, pondlike pool rimmed with great misshapen boulders. The trout liked the easy stir of the current below its impact with the boulder, and three or four held well up along its soft edges.

At first, my Anatomical *Baetis*/PMD nymph drifting a few inches below a dry fly hooked a couple of fish. Then the duns began showing in earnest, and

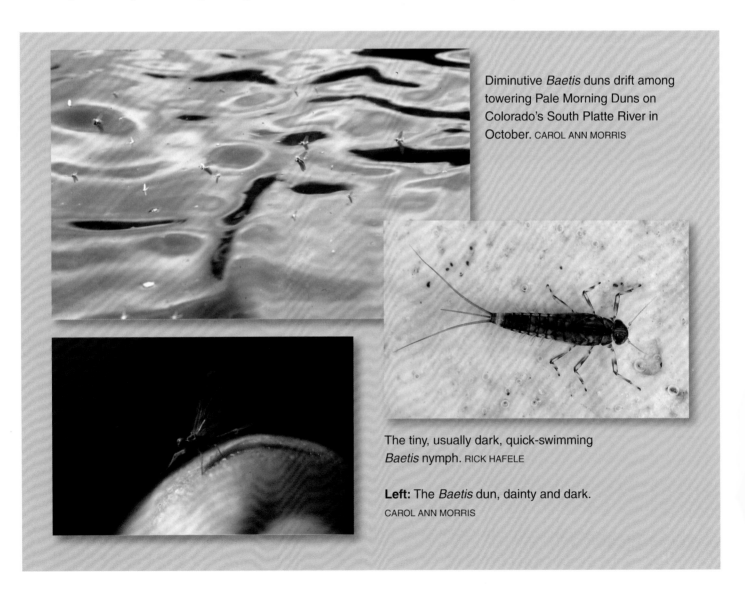

Diminutive *Baetis* duns drift among towering Pale Morning Duns on Colorado's South Platte River in October. CAROL ANN MORRIS

The tiny, usually dark, quick-swimming *Baetis* nymph. RICK HAFELE

**Left:** The *Baetis* dun, dainty and dark.
CAROL ANN MORRIS

Heavy morning fog surrounds a trout stream in fall—pray it holds through the afternoon *Baetis* hatch. CAROL ANN MORRIS

the fish seemed to demand an emerger or full dry fly accurately placed and perfectly drifted. I put on a tiny *Baetis* Sparkle Dun and had hooked several more trout when things changed again.

Pale Morning Dun mayflies, small themselves yet towering over the *Baetis* duns, began as an occasional whitish anomaly and then built rapidly to a real hatch as *Baetis* withdrew. Mid-October in most places in the West is late for PMDs, so I was surprised to see them at all, much less in respectable numbers. I put on an early version of my Morris Emerger, PMD and went back to hooking trout— whenever I got my cast and drift just so—until the icy sting of high-elevation autumn sundown drove us out. I landed nothing over 15 inches, but nothing under a foot either. Mostly trim, healthy, beautiful browns and a few rainbows. A dozen good fish lost and a dozen landed. By my reckoning, a fine day on most any trout river.

A strong showing of PMDs counts as an anomaly over my years of October fishing. But I've consistently found October a fine month for *Baetis*. Actually, *Baetis* can hatch any month of the year, so you'd be wise to always watch for it. The thing is, this little mayfly really steals the show (at least so far as mayflies are concerned) during the cold months, which makes *Baetis* primarily a three-season mayfly. But I associate it mainly with just one period: real fall. That's because I've done most of my *Baetis* fishing in late September through October. And often, it's been very good, sometimes plain wonderful.

But other mayflies aren't the only insects hatching from trout rivers in fall, winter, and early spring alongside *Baetis* or within hours of its hatch. Oregon's Deschutes and Montana's Bitterroot rivers, among many others in the West, offer the massive October Caddis on chilly autumn days, and many Western streams provide midday emergences of several small winter stones. Hefty *Skwala* stoneflies scurry across some Western rivers in late winter. But for top-water action during the chilly to icy months across the North American continent, minuscule

# Skip Morris

CAROL ANN MORRIS

**Right:** The female *Baetis* spinner, often overlooked by fly fishers, seldom by trout. RICK HAFELE

midges are probably *Baetis*'s chief competition. So prepare for them too. But some off-season days are midge days, some are *Baetis* days, and some days are both, with the mayflies typically providing the first action and the midges following. Only a fool would ignore either insect during the off-season.

Fall, winter, and on into spring is no easy time for the fly fisher. Wet hands and numb flesh are the norm, thanks to wind, rain, snow, and general cold. But *Baetis* holds a powerful attraction for those anglers who can't bear to put their rods away just because days turn sour in late autumn. It's a clean-hatching mayfly, wriggling up openly as a nymph to split its shuck, free its wings, rise proudly erect on its feet with wings held high, and enjoy a leisurely ride atop the current beneath the gloomy skies it loves. Fortunately for the fly fisher, the mayfly's ride up in the air may be short; a midday trout often comes up to meet the delicate insect, drawing it down in a gentle sip and—best of all—a predictable rhythm. Getting

a fly to drift naturally and free, to follow the right line of current so that it comes right up to the trout, to arrive at that moment when the trout hits the rise-point of its feeding pattern—all this becomes a fly fisher's game of quiet fascination . . . That is, until the hook is set. Then things liven up considerably.

By now, this should be clear: If you're going to fish outside the mild, easy, standard trout season on rivers, or even at the early and late ends of that season (actually, if you're going to fish trout rivers at all), you need to know *Baetis*. So, here goes . . .

---

**Opposite page:** Snow is fine with the BWO.
CAROL ANN MORRIS

Sunny days may condense the *Baetis* hatch and put the trout on edge, but such days can nonetheless provide good action. CAROL ANN MORRIS

The *Baetis* mayfly, also known as the Blue-Winged Olive and by the acronym BWO, can, and under good conditions often does, hatch in abundance. Of course it can also hatch from steady moderation down to just the occasional drifting emerger or dun, any of which may be enough to interest trout during the lean, cold months when the nymphs and larvae of most insect species lie hidden, waiting for warmer times for their emergence.

The best *Baetis* hatches have always come for me in lousy weather—overcast for starters, and if there's wind and rain or snow, all the better for the hatch. Personally, though, I'm fine with just the overcast and a steady hatch—I hate wind. On sunny days, the hatch can be strong but will probably be short, and the trout may show little enthusiasm for exposing themselves at the surface of the river where predators can target their illuminated bodies.

The *Baetis* nymph is trim and tiny, ranging from overall light olive to dark brown, occasionally gray. It

has three tails, but a short center tail (a few species have only two tails). It's an agile swimmer, so you'd expect that ability to serve it in quick currents, yet *Baetis* seems happy in all sorts of slow to swift water—runs, flats, riffles, pools—which may in part explain why so many rivers offer good hatches.

Fishing an imitation of the *Baetis* nymph is always a reasonable tactic all through the day whenever the mayfly is active. Just before the hatch—as early as 11:00 a.m. to as late as 2:00 p.m. during the cool and cold months—can be an especially promising time to fish a nymph down along the riverbed below a strike indicator. But in the heat of a hatch, I've sometimes made a dramatic leap from slow fishing with a dry fly or emerger to fast fishing by switching to a tiny dark nymph dangled on 8 or 10 inches of tippet from the bend of the dry fly's hook and passed through the rises. (I recall a day on Alberta's Crowsnest with this rig when a half hour of refusals with a dry fly during the *Baetis* hatch only sweetened the next hour of constant strikes to a size 18 nymph inches deep.)

"Blue-Winged Olive" is as much a description of the *Baetis* dun as it is a title. There is a quality of blue in the slate-colored wings, and the underside of the dun, the part trout see, is usually some kind of olive, ranging from pale to dark, and sometimes shaded with gray, brown, or tan. The dun has two tails and uncommonly tiny hind wings. Unlike most mayfly species with small but significant secondary wings nestled alongside the primary ones, the hind wings of *Baetis* are infinitesimal, almost invisible to the unaided eye, and sometimes absent altogether.

Emergers and dry flies are the standard once the hatch is in full swing. They're normally fished dead-drift out among the rising fish. A feeding trout won't stray far for a tiny *Baetis* dun, so expect to make accurate casts and accurate drifts of your flies. Sometimes, though, *Baetis* duns flutter and flip around out there on the water, and I suspect the trout notice. So

I've been experimenting with twitching my floating imitations. No real conclusions yet, but keep this option in your pocket as you fish the hatch.

The female *Baetis* spinner returns to the water to release her eggs, and then, atop the river, she fails. Her wings fall to gravity, her legs curl inward as though clutching death. Flat on the water she is plain to trout but difficult for anglers to detect. You'll have to put your nose down close to find her, and you may not find her, since on some streams she breaks her midday to evening egg-laying habit by performing the task at night. When you do find her, try showing the fish any reliable BWO spinner pattern, dead-drift.

Don't expect to hear much about fishing *Baetis* spinnerfalls, though. The spinner—precisely, I suspect, because she's so easy to miss—is customarily overlooked by fly fishers. But trout know she's easy prey. They feed upon her lazily, making only the quietest of rises in the slow water.

Spinners of *Baetis* have the characteristic clear wings of most mayfly spinners and the two tails of the dun. The underside of the body typically runs from olive-brown to dark reddish brown. Many

---

**Below:** Fishing on the edge during the Blue-Winged Olive hatch. CAROL ANN MORRIS

# Skip Morris

varieties of mayfly pick up this red-brown coloring in their spinner stage—fly fishers call it "rust"—so there are plenty of spinner patterns out there that use it in their bodies.

*Baetis* is the hatch I see and will always see first in my mind whenever I think of off-season—especially fall—trout fishing on rivers. It's a fine hatch, offering all the challenge and opportunity any real fly fisher could want. And it's generously distributed across Canada and the United States, so if you live in trout country, you probably won't have to look far to find it.

**ANATOMICAL *BAETIS*/PMD**

*Skip Morris*

CAROL ANN MORRIS

**Hook:** #14-20 heavy wire, short to 1X long
**Bead (optional):** Black metal, $\frac{5}{64}$-inch for size 14 hooks, $\frac{1}{16}$-inch for size 16 and smaller
**Weight (optional):** Fine copper wire
**Thread:** Brown 8/0
**Tail:** Three pheasant-tail fibers, split with thread turns, or 2 split tails
**Rib:** Gold wire, wound opposite the normal direction
**Abdomen:** Pheasant tail
**Wing Case:** Brown Stretch Flex, Medallion sheeting, or Thin Skin
**Legs:** Olive-dyed partridge or hen back
**Thorax:** Olive-brown rabbit fur

**Notes:** I bind the leg fibers to stand upright, almost as a wing; then I push them out to the sides and press them at the center with closed scissor blades to crease them. The wing case, pulled over the top of the thorax, holds the fibers splayed out to the sides. The bead is optional, but it sure helps the fly descend. Without the bead, you can add tiny barbell eyes; make them by melting the ends of a short length of monofilament.

Nymphs of *Baetis* and Pale Morning Dun mayflies are so similar in color, form, and size that this fairly detailed nymph dressing convincingly imitates them both.

**BLM, PEACOCK**

*Tim Heng*

CAROL ANN MORRIS

**Hook:** #16-20 heavy wire, standard length
**Thread:** Olive 8/0
**Rib:** Fine copper wire
**Thorax:** Copper metal bead, $\frac{5}{64}$-inch diameter for size 20, $\frac{3}{32}$-inch for sizes 18 and 20
**Tail, Abdomen, Wing Case, and Legs:** Peacock Angel Hair or Lite Brite

**Notes:** This is one flashy little nymph. Sometimes flashy is just right. Slip the bead on first. Bind on the rib. Make the tails from a few strands of Angel Hair or Lite Brite. These strands are wound to make the abdomen, and then the rib wire is spiraled up it. Next, the thread is whip-finished and cut and then restarted in front of the bead. The strands are pulled over the top of the bead for the wing case and bound in front, and the ends of the strands are bound, divided back, and trimmed for legs.

**MORRIS EMERGER, BWO**

*Skip Morris*

| | |
|---|---|
| **Hook:** | #16-22 light wire, curved shank (pupa/emerger hook) |
| **Thread:** | Olive 8/0 |
| **Tail:** | Brown mottled hen saddle |
| **Abdomen:** | Dark brown rabbit |
| **Thorax:** | Buoyant olive dubbing |

**Wing and Burst Shuck:** Natural dark coastal deer hair

**Notes:** The hair is bound only with a narrow collar of thread directly in front of the thorax, so leave plenty of room in front of the thorax for the wing. A couple of tight layers of thread provide a solid grip for the wing. The hair wing is essentially the Compara-dun wing, a fan of hair tips, but angling slightly forward. The blunt-cut butts of the hair suggest the burst shuck where the wings emerged. Floatant rubbed into these butts really holds the fly afloat. The Morris Emerger can be tied in other colors and sizes to imitate the Western Green Drake, *Callibaetis*, the Pale Morning Dun, and just about any other mayfly.

Morris Emergers are mainly what I fish now for PMD and *Baetis* hatches. Leave out a fly I trust and regularly fish? That seemed dishonest. So, lucky you—you get two! You also get two photos of the fly because a side view alone suggests it's really just a Quigley Cripple without the hackle when, in fact, it's more like a Compara-dun than a Quigley. Really, I borrowed from both flies to come up with one that is neither, a blend of each design's best qualities.

**NO-HACKLE, GRAY/OLIVE**

*Doug Swisher and Carl Richards*

| | |
|---|---|
| **Hook:** | #16-22 light wire, standard length to 1X long, sizes 22 to 16 |
| **Thread:** | Olive 8/0 |
| **Tail:** | Gray (or medium blue dun) hackle fibers, split |
| **Abdomen:** | Buoyant olive dubbing (or dyed rabbit) |
| **Wings:** | Duck primary sections |
| **Thorax:** | Same as the abdomen |

**Notes:** The No-Hackle, looking naked in its stark outline next to the brushy hackle-bearing flies of the day, leapt to popularity soon after *Selective Trout* came out back in 1971. It remains a standard fly for difficult trout on smooth, clear water.

**KRYSTAL WING BWO SPINNER**

*Scott Sanchez*

| | |
|---|---|
| **Hook:** | #14-20 light wire, 1X long |
| **Thread:** | Light gray 8/0 |
| **Tail:** | Split gray Microfibetts |
| **Abdomen:** | Fine brown dubbing |
| **Wing:** | Pearl Krystal Flash over clear Antron |
| **Thorax:** | Peacock color dubbing |

   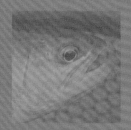

# Winter

This fat rainbow took a size 18 Krystal Flash BWO Nymph after ignoring larger, more appetizing (to me) stonefly nymphs.

*Rick Hafele*

# Winter Bugs and Nymph Fishing

In some ways there is no better time to fish nymphs than winter. You know the usual quote: *Nymphs make up 70 to 80 percent of a trout's diet*. Well, in the winter that number goes up. I'm not sure by how much, but given that there are few hatches and fewer to no terrestrial insects to eat, trout have little left to eat but nymphs. Another reason nymphs matter in the winter is that most aquatic insects are at their greatest abundance as nymphs or larvae during the winter. Thus when hatches and terrestrial insects are at their lowest numbers, nymphs and larvae are at their highest. The end result is that for most successful winter trout fishing you will need to fish nymphs.

Air temp, 28 degrees. Water temp? Damn cold! RICK HAFELE

Because the greatest abundance of nymphs occur in the winter, a healthy trout stream has a wide variety of nymphs for trout to choose from. Sometimes this means just about any buggy looking nymph pattern will catch fish. But it can also mean that if trout have a lot to choose from, they get picky. So just because the water's cold and you have ice in your guides, don't expect the trout to fall over themselves for just any old fly you throw to them.

Just as in other seasons I like to have some idea of what type of aquatic insects are abundant when I'm fishing in the winter, so I still take a little time to sample the bugs in the stream and look for clues for what would be most available for trout to eat. Mostly I look for insects I know are active and likely to be drifting in the current. At the top of this list are mayflies with swimming nymphs. The most important of these are the Blue-Winged Olives (family Baetidae, genus *Baetis*). These little guys can be plentiful throughout the winter, and because they are active swimmers they end up drifting in the current—a lot. Trout feeding studies also show that trout have a high preference for *Baetis* nymphs whenever they are present. So when I see a lot of Blue-Winged Olive (BWO) nymphs, the Krystal Flash BWO nymph is my first choice.

might be tempted to tie these in sizes you can actually see, remember to pick a pattern that matches the size of the naturals where you are fishing. They are never big!

The other mayfly nymph in my winter selection is the Bead-head Pale Morning Dun or PMD. In many ways this fly looks a lot like a Bead-head Hare's Ear Nymph, another effective pattern. And like the Hare's Ear it resembles a variety of different natural nymphs. While this fly is called a PMD, in the winter the real PMDs are small and not as important as they will be in late spring and early summer. This fly pattern, therefore, is more likely imitating other mayflies such as the March Brown nymph (family Heptageniidae, genus *Rhithrogena*) that matures in late winter. I also tie this fly without the wing case. The result is a fly that looks a lot like a caddis pupa as well as a mayfly nymph. While caddis hatches aren't likely in the winter, as you move into March several different caddis hatches start, and one of the best is the *Glossosoma* or Turtle-Case Caddis. The pupae of these guys are roughly size 16 or 18, and this fly does a reasonable job of matching them.

I most often fish this fly the same way I do the BWO: near the bottom with a dead-drift presentation using a floating line, strike indicator, and split shot as needed to get to the bottom. If I know caddis are hatching, I will let it sink and then use the rod to lift it back up toward the surface, a.k.a. a Leisenring Lift. If you are using it specifically to imitate a rising caddis pupa, you can do away with the strike indicator, but you will probably still need a split shot on the tippet to sink it a couple feet deep unless you are fishing in very slow-moving water.

Caddis larvae are also abundant during the winter months. Some of the most numerous are net-spinning caddis (family Hydropsychidae, genus *Hydropsyche* and *Cheumatopsyche*) and free-living Green Rock Worms (family Rhyacophilidae, genus *Rhyacophila*). The Krystal Flash Green Rock Worm Nymph is tied to specifically match a Green Rock Worm larva, but many species of net-spinning caddis larvae are also bright green. This nymph, therefore, does a good job of imitating a wide range of available caddis larvae. You can easily change the body color if you find that bright green isn't exactly what you want for your area.

I almost always fish this pattern with the classic shot-and-indicator approach. The naturals don't swim, so they drift with little or no movement close

I think the keys to this little nymph are its slender silhouette, flashy body, buggy thorax, and sinkability, meaning the materials it is tied with help it sink. As a bonus it's also easy to tie and is durable.

You might find a BWO hatch in the winter, but more likely you'll just find nymphs in the drift. This means you'll want to fish the fly close to the stream bottom, and while the nymphs are good swimmers, in most situations letting your fly drift naturally with the current will be most effective. At the tail end of each cast you can twitch the fly for a little more action.

Size is important. These are small mayflies, and I have consistently found that a size 18 imitation will out-fish a size 14 almost every time. Thus, while you

Winter nymphing will hone your nymph-fishing skills for the rest of the season.

to the streambed. The shot-and-indicator method matches this behavior quite well. If you are fishing a stream where you can wade close to the water, high-sticking and Czech nymphing methods also work well. Like most winter nymphing, strikes will usually be soft, so any method that improves your ability to feel or see strikes is better.

The last nymph in my winter lineup is the Golden Stone Nymph. This great searching nymph pattern is effective all year. Golden Stone nymphs (family Perlidae) require two to three years to mature, which means nymphs are present in different stages all the time. It also means that most nymphs are not the large (size 6, 3XL), fully mature nymphs that hatch in late May through July. Most nymphs are considerably smaller and best imitated with patterns in sizes 10 to 12. That's what I like to use in the winter: a size 10 or 12 3XL Golden Stone Nymph.

The naturals are voracious predators and actively crawl around on the stream bottom in search of little mayflies, midges, and caddis larvae to eat. While active, they are not good swimmers and when drifting in the current they tend to glide and tumble until they bump into a rock to grab onto. Thus, getting your nymph close to the bottom and letting it drift naturally with the current is the best approach.

One of my favorite nymphing setups is to use two nymphs with the Golden Stone first and then a small mayfly or caddis nymph tied onto a 15- to 20-inch dropper attached to the hook bend of the Golden Stone. It often seems that two nymphs out-fish a single nymph, so it is definitely worth a try. (Note: Fishing two flies at once is illegal in some areas—check the fishing regulations first!)

**KRYSTAL FLASH BLUE-WINGED OLIVE**

*Rick Hafele*

**Hook:** #16-18, 1X short scud hook
**Thread:** Tan 8/0
**Tails:** Four to eight tan hackle fibers
**Body:** Four to six strands of Krystal Flash twisted together to form rope
**Wing Case:** Same as body
**Thorax and Legs:** Pine squirrel dubbing with guard hairs

**BEAD-HEAD PALE MORNING DUN**

*Rick Hafele*

**Hook:** #12-16, 1X short scud hook
**Head:** Gold bead
**Thread:** Brown 6/0 or 8/0
**Tails:** Three to six brown hen hackle fibers
**Rib:** Copper wire
**Body:** Brown nymph dubbing
**Wing Case (optional):** Dark gray or black goose
**Thorax:** Pine squirrel spun in dubbing loop

**KRYSTAL FLASH GREEN ROCK WORM**

*Rick Hafele*

**Hook:** #10-14, 2X long nymph hook
**Head:** Gold bead
**Weight:** Twelve turns non-lead wire, diameter of hook shank
**Thread:** Green 6/0 or 8/0
**Body:** Four to six strands of green Krystal Flash twisted together to form rope
**Thorax:** Pine squirrel fur spun in dubbing loop
**Notes:** These two flies fished in tandem is one of my favorite nymph-fishing combinations.

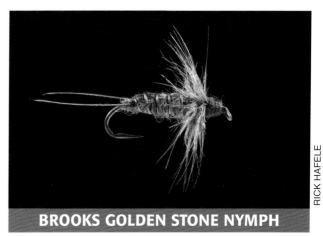

**BROOKS GOLDEN STONE NYMPH**

*Charles Brooks with slight modifications by Rick Hafele*

**Hook:** #10-12, 3X long
**Weight:** Twelve to fifteen turns non-lead wire, diameter of hook shank
**Thread:** Black 6/0 or 8/0
**Tails:** Two pheasant-tail fibers
**Rib:** Copper wire
**Body:** Medium brown dubbing
**Shellback:** Turkey tail section pulled over top of body
**Thorax:** Two to four turns of brown hen hackle
**Head:** Reddish brown dubbing
**Notes:** I use other nymph patterns as well depending on specific situations, but these four consistently find themselves attached to the end of my leader.

When the air and water are both cold and no signs of life—insect or trout—show on the surface, your best bet for engaging in some action will be to fish nymphs down near the bottom. DAVE HUGHES

# Dave Hughes

# Winter Nymphs

It's a throwaway line that you fish during the bitter part of the year with streamers and nymphs large enough that trout can see them down there, that are big enough to motivate trout into moving against their best instincts to conserve energy. You fish these flies right on the bottom, cast them over and over, don't expect a strike until your toes are frozen, your fingers are so brittle some of them get knocked off when you accidentally bump the rod, and your nose has an icicle hanging down so far it interferes with the feeble workings of what's left of your line hand. But fishing, surprisingly, reflects the nature of the angler, and not all anglers are so desirous of catching trout that they'll fish in such rotten conditions.

Cold water and cold air can make for cold fishing. But there are still fish to be caught. If one pattern doesn't work try another. Try fishing slower water than you might otherwise fish. Experiment until you feel that tug on the end of your line! RICK HAFELE

The first thing we have to do, when trying to decide what flies might become our winter favorites, is to assess our own willingness to fight nature in our pursuit of a few trout to fight. There are those of us, and I might or might not confess to being among them, who would rather watch for stretches of winter weather that are more civilized, that allow fishing that is at least slightly comparable to what we do during the rest of the year; and who insist we enjoy our time out there.

Rivers and streams are often as low and clear in winter as they are at any other time of year. If high and cloudy water are eliminated as differences in the fishing, a couple of major variations still remain. First, the water is almost certain to be colder, therefore the fish less active, and second, insects are far

less likely to be hatching, causing trout to be, once again, less active, because they have less to be active about. Aside from a consequent lack of willingness to chase flies very far to take them, this couple of causes results in a pair of outcomes. First, trout hold in somewhat "softer" water than they do at other times of year, where they have less current to fight, and second, they lose some of their territorial instincts and tend to be bunched up rather than sprinkled over a broadcast set of lies.

So the major change you might find it necessary to make in winter fishing, as opposed to spring, summer, and fall fishing, is in the way you read the water. If trout are concentrated, and you fish where they're not located, it's unlikely that you'll catch them no matter the fly you fish. Make your first major change, when fishing winter instead of warmer parts of the year, a change in the way you read the water. It's not necessarily the subject of this piece, but learn to look for places where it looks like trout might be comfortable, and that you might not focus your fishing when it's warmer, and see if you can't locate some trout down there. If you find one, it's likely you will have found a bunch.

Given that change, then how do you select a small set of winter flies, and as an important corollary, how do you fish them?

My main criteria for nymphs selected for fishing in winter is confidence in the fly. Conditions are inherently tougher. The prospects for catching trout are slightly to significantly diminished. I would not consider rigging a nymph to the end of my tippet that has not provided lots of success for me, at other times of year, and preferably, at all times of year.

So the answer becomes simple: My favorite winter nymphs are the same ones I use most often in all other parts of the year. I have a narrow set of flies I use when conditions fail to point to the use of anything specific. In winter I encounter the highest proportion of those sorts of conditions. So I'm nearly always armed with my most dependable nymphs, with one or more often two of those dressings that do the most to enliven my expectations. Rather than switching to a set of nymphs specific to winter, I fall back on flies that I find most effective at all times of year.

The first criteria in your own selection of winter nymphs, then, should be to use those that you have the most confidence in, and that have caught the most trout for you, no matter the time of year or conditions on the stream or river. Don't use anything I'm going to suggest here unless you haven't developed your own set of favorites. I promise you that if you already have flies that you think are going to catch trout whenever you get them into water, those flies are going to work better for you than my flies, in winter or any other season—nymphs, drys, or any other kind of flies.

Given that, it's wise in winter to have a small set of nymphs that cover the color and size spectrums: large, medium, small, and tiny; dark, drab, moderate, and shiny. That way you can offer trout all sorts of choices, to see which they prefer on any given winter day.

## Darrel Martin

I read all of Darrel Martin's books when they came out, most devoutly *Fly-Tying Methods* and *Micropatterns*, but over the years I got away from their lessons. About a year ago I was on the track of something and went into Darrel again because so many trails in fly tying lead to his books. I decided to reread him, all of him that I could find. And I realized that I'd missed something in Darrel the first time. He spends a lot of time in Europe, so he's into a lot of innovations that are made over there, and over here as well, before they trickle down to where the rest of us become aware of them: bead heads, CDC, etc. In fact, Darrel is very often the agent of that trickling down of information, through his books and through his articles in *Fly Rod & Reel* magazine, for which he was long fly-tying columnist and is still a fly-tying contributor.

But I already knew that about him. What I'd missed was behind that. Darrel is also very cognizant of fly-tying history. The more I read his books the more I realized that Darrel is a bridge between fly tying's history and fly tying's future. He fuses knowledge of traditions—methods both well-known and obscure—with knowledge of what's on the cutting edge. He has a brilliant mind, has encyclopedic knowledge of flies and fly tying, and is a fine writer. If you haven't read Darrel Martin, you've missed a deeply satisfying treat, and at the same time a highly valuable education. ■

My own favorites follow. If you catch me nymphing, at any time of year, you'll probably find one of them, possibly in combination with another of them, or with something else more dependent on the specific situation, tied in tandem to my tippet. Some, but not all, of the following flies are listed, with tying instructions, in my book *Nymphs for Streams and Stillwaters*.

# Dave Hughes

**SALMONFLY SIMPLICITY**

*Dave Hughes*

DAVE HUGHES

**LIGHTNING BUG**

*Larry Graham*

DAVE HUGHES

| | |
|---|---|
| **Hook:** | #6-12, 3X long |
| **Head:** | Black tungsten bead |
| **Weight:** | Fifteen turns non-lead wire, diameter of hook shank |
| **Thread:** | Black 3/0 or 6/0 |
| **Tails:** | Black biots, forked |
| **Abdomen:** | Mix of 2 parts black rabbit fur, 1 part rust and 1 part charcoal sparkle yarn |
| **Gills:** | White ostrich herl |
| **Legs:** | Black rubber legs |
| **Thorax:** | Same as abdomen |

**Notes:** This is a corruption of Charles Brooks's Montana Stone. The original works at least as well, probably better, but this is how mine has evolved. Both the original and my version have captured a lot of trout for me—confidence! I tie and fish them more often in sizes 10 and 12 than I do in 6 and 8. It's my most common big nymph to use in a two-fly combo.

| | |
|---|---|
| **Hook:** | #12-16, 1X long |
| **Head:** | Gold bead |
| **Weight:** | Twelve turns non-lead wire, diameter of hook shank |
| **Thread:** | Black 6/0 or 8/0 |
| **Tails:** | Pheasant-tail fibers |
| **Rib:** | Fine copper wire |
| **Body:** | Flat pearlescent or holographic Mylar |
| **Wing Case:** | Same as body |
| **Thorax:** | Peacock herl |
| **Legs:** | Hen back fibers |

**Notes:** This is obviously the bright nymph in my box. I've had terrific luck on it at times on winter streams, usually in size 14 or 16. I had never tried it until I was researching *Nymphs for Streams and Stillwaters*. The Lightning Bug took tying a dozen to work out the steps for photos. I stuck that dozen in my nymph box, tried them first on Owyhee River brown trout in winter. It worked such wonders that it jumped instantly into my stable as my bright fly and has caught so many trout since then, in such a wide variety of situations, that it remains there.

**PINK SQUIRREL**

*DAVE HUGHES*

*John Bethke*

| | |
|---|---|
| **Hook:** | #12-16, 1X long |
| **Head:** | Gold bead |
| **Weight:** | Ten turns non-lead wire, diameter of hook shank |
| **Thread:** | Tan 8/0 |
| **Tail:** | Pine squirrel guard hairs |
| **Abdomen:** | ½ pine squirrel fur, ½ beige Sparkle Yarn |
| **Thorax:** | Pink rabbit fur (Hareline #04) |

**Notes:** This is my simplification of John Bethke's original Pink Squirrel. He's a guide and professional tier from Wisconsin. He sent me a dozen of his tie, and it was so effective on my home Deschutes, and everywhere else that I've used it, that I was almost astounded by it. I fish it a lot, usually in size 16, most often as the small fly behind the Salmonfly Simplicity, but also at times as the medium fly above a Pheasant Tail. I highly recommend you contact John and order some of his flies rather than use my bastardized version; you'll catch more fish with it: John Bethke, Westby, WI; QJLB@yahoo.com.

**PHEASANT TAIL**

*DAVE HUGHES*

*Frank Sawyer*

| | |
|---|---|
| **Hook:** | #16-20, 1X long |
| **Thread:** | XS Copper Ultra Wire |
| **Tail:** | Pheasant-tail fibers |
| **Body:** | Pheasant-tail fibers |

**Notes:** This is another one that I discovered while working on the research for *Nymphs for Streams and Stillwaters*. I decided to back away from the Pheasant Tail as we tie it, either as a flashback or with pheasant tail for the thorax, in Al Troth's popular version. Both, by the way, are remarkably effective winter nymphs. But I wanted to learn to tie it with copper wire, as originator Frank Sawyer did on the Dove and other British chalkstreams. It took a long time to work out the proper proportions; my best source became the great Darrel Martin's book *Fly-Tying Methods*.

You can get the right size wire for this nymph by stripping #18 electrical wire. The original Sawyer tie turned out to have the right brightness, density, and shape to fish perfectly for me, winter, spring, summer, and fall, and especially when small Blue-Winged Olive (*Baetis*) nymphs are active, which they are, more often than most other insects, in the winter of our fly-fishing season.

Winter trout flies come in a great range of sizes and styles. SKIP MORRIS

Skip Morris

# Selecting Flies for Winter Trout

Now in my sixties, I'm no fan of icy fishing. What used to be merely uncomfortable (even *unnoticeable* when the fish were busy distracting me) has become almost painful—stinging cheeks, numb toes, and worst of all wet hands chilled so deeply that they fumble to tie on a fly. But after a few weeks mostly cooped up by a Christmas-card fire of diminishing charm and living within the confines of a few rooms, I dream of trout bouncing against my fly rod. I know that with good timing and perhaps (though not necessarily) a bit of travel, this dream can be realized even in the dead of winter.

# Skip Morris

CAROL ANN MORRIS

Consequently I end up fishing a few times from November through March every year. I rarely regret it. For one thing, I live in a place where there are no good excuses for letting a winter pass unfished—the winter months are mild, seldom freezing, and the trout lakes and sea-run cutthroat beaches can be good even in the coldest months if the weather allows. But in most places across the United States and Canada, winter lakes may offer something to the ice fisher and the ice skater but nothing to the fly fisher—and sea-run cutthroat trout are just faraway mysteries. But winter rivers are another matter.

Usually combined with a speaking tour, I sample winter trout rivers every year across North America. Again, numb hands, no regrets. Such travel has convinced me that throughout most of the United States and Canada there is some sort of river fishing for trout year round. If you live in a really frigid state or Canadian province where winter river fishing is hopeless, you can always escape south for a chance to work a trout fly in the currents. Have a relative or close friend in Colorado or New Mexico or California you could visit for the holidays? If so, pack a couple of four-section rods and the rest and go.

Nearly all the winter trout fishing I've found in rivers was about fishing a nymph dead-drift or an emerger or dry fly to a hatch of Blue-Winged Olive mayflies, midges, or, rarely, winter stoneflies. Too rarely, really, for me to say much about the stones (though I've occasionally had some fast fishing with them).

When I choose a nymph for winter fishing, I face the same broad choice I face any time of year: imitation or attractor. My sensible approach to imitative nymphs is to try to show the trout something familiar. For example, if I know a river gets a big hatch of Golden Stoneflies in summer, I'm likely to fish a large imitation of a Golden Stone nymph in winter simply because so many are around that I figure the trout are used to seeing them and watching for them. Rocks tumble, due to high water or the constant settling of a streambed, which can send a few nymphs off to waiting trout, and at any time nymphs can make mistakes that get them swept away. There are fine points to this business, however.

The massive Golden Stonefly takes two or three years to mature. This means that some middle-agers are down there, each offering a substantial bite for a trout. So an insect that takes more than a year to mature—especially a *big* insect—is a fine candidate for imitation in winter, even if the insect won't hatch for months. But imitating a PMD mayfly nymph in

# Skip Morris

# Techniques for River Trout in Winter

No matter how unseasonably pleasant the day, winter rivers are cold and cold-blooded trout will be sluggish, so don't expect them to dart to your fly. If you're fishing a nymph, get it deep and drifting free with the current, dead-drift. Since you may have to get it closer to a trout than you would in summer, be thorough—make plenty of casts and try to drift the fly through all the good holding water repeatedly. It may even take a couple of close passes of the fly to move a lethargic fish. Same with a streamer—slow and deep with lots of casts.

Use a dry fly or emerger only if the fish are rising. You may have to drift the fly right into a fish rather than just near it. But on the whole, rising winter trout are in feeding mode and more active than they'll be the rest of the day. So on the whole, fish the dry fly or emerger in winter about as you would in the summer, just a little more accurately and patiently. ▪

January makes no sense to me. The nymph matures in only a year, so in winter it's still really tiny. Too tiny. If trout in low water or a quiet tailwater or spring creek seem to want a tiny nymph, I'll give them one. But I'm not worried about imitating specifically a pinpoint baby PMD nymph.

Insects that hatch early in the season are another matter. March Brown mayfly nymphs (which can hatch as early as February) will be of good size in midwinter, and an imitation may well be worth a try.

Attractors? Any of them to me are fair game in winter, or any other time of year. I tend to reach for my Gabriel's Trumpet out of habit, in gold or pink or brown or purple. It's caught me so many trout under so many conditions I always tie it on with confidence. But no fly is a consistent sure thing. So try a Flashback Pheasant Tail or a Rainbow Warrior—it's hard to know what design and color of attractor will work best, so just keep trying new ones until the fish come.

Whatever nymph you fish in winter, fish it deep and dead-drift—drowsy winter trout won't move far for your fly with cold-thickened blood creeping through their bodies.

Emergers and dry flies aren't normally worth much in winter without a hatch. *With* a hatch, they can be great fun. Midwinter hatches usually come off when the water reaches its highest temperature of the day, sometime in the afternoon. During a spate of unusually warm weather, they can start earlier. Since I encounter winter Blue-Winged Olives and midges over and over—the little stuff—I'll keep to them here. I still fall back on the old standard for midges: the Griffith's Gnat. It's easy to tie, so I can turn out a bunch of 20s, 22s, and 24s in pretty short order. Sometimes I tie 24s and 26s, because sometimes that's what it takes to effectively imitate the smaller specimens. As I said, little stuff. But if there are enough of them on the water—and midges typically do hatch in abundance—lethargic winter trout will usually rise to sip them. There are other good flies for this work. If the fish are refusing the Gnat, I'll try a midge pupa imitation, such as the Mercury Black Beauty, perhaps just a few inches under the river's surface.

For winter *Baetis* (Blue-Winged Olive) mayflies I use my Morris Emerger, BWO, but a Compara-dun or Gulper Special or RS2 in size 20 or 18 will serve honorably. As with the Griffith's Gnat, I just throw it upstream of a rising trout with sufficient slack in line and leader, mend if I must, and watch for a take.

I've caught winter trout on streamers, but seldom, though often enough that I know these flies can work. The last time I pulled this off was with a good old-fashioned Black Ghost twitched down deep in a spring creek. I guess it just swung too close to those trout lying quietly down on the riverbed and looked too good to pass up. That's not much to offer on winter streamer fishing, but it's what I have. Obviously, I'm really a midwinter nymph/emerger/dry-fly man.

If the happy distraction of the holidays isn't enough to keep your mind off fishing or you tire of the long nights and indoor life of winter, watch for a mild day and, when one comes, head out to a trout river. You'll likely have no regrets once the day is done.

Nymph patterns (clockwise from top): Bird's Stonefly Nymph, Mercury Black Beauty, Hackled Skip Nymph, and Gabriel's Trumpet, Gold. SKIP MORRIS

## BIRD'S STONEFLY NYMPH

*Cal Bird*

| | |
|---|---|
| **Hook:** | #4-10 heavy wire, 3X long |
| **Thread:** | Orange 8/0, 6/0, or 3/0 |
| **Weight:** | Lead or lead-substitute wire |
| **Tails:** | Dyed-brown goose biots |
| **Rib:** | Orange floss or heavy thread |
| **Abdomen:** | Brown muskrat fur or dyed-brown rabbit fur |
| **Wing Case:** | Dark mottled turkey primary or dyed-brown teal |
| **Legs:** | One furnace or brown saddle hackle, spiraled over the thorax |
| **Thorax:** | Peacock herl |

## MERCURY BLACK BEAUTY

*Pat Dorsey*

| | |
|---|---|
| **Hook:** | #18-24 heavy wire (or standard to light wire), short shank to standard length |
| **Bead:** | One tiny crystal (clear) bead |
| **Thread:** | Black 8/0 |
| **Rib:** | Fine copper (I often substitute silver) wire |
| **Abdomen:** | Black working thread |

**Notes:** Pat's original dressing includes a collar of black Super Fine Dry Fly dubbing, which I normally replace with a buildup of the working thread that I coat with head cement, as I did with the fly in the photo. The variations of rib and thorax in the dressing above came from my word-of-mouth introduction to the Mercury Black Beauty while fishing for a full October on Colorado's South Platte River—one of the rivers of its birth. The fly was rising into the chatter of local fly fishers back then and that chatter offered several versions. I picked the features I liked from the lot and behold—the fly in the photo above appeared in my tying vise. It works. In fact I came to trust it for those infuriating South Platte trout.

# Skip Morris

## BEAD HEAD HACKLED SKIP NYMPH (MARCH BROWN VERSION)

*Skip Morris*

**Hook:** #12-14 heavy wire, 2X long
**Bead:** Black, brown, or copper metal
**Weight:** 0.015-inch lead or lead-substitute wire
**Thread:** Brown 6/0 or 8/0
**Rib:** Small copper wire
**Abdomen:** Tan to brown rabbit fur
**Back and Tails:**
**Legs:** Tan hen back (saddle) hackle
**Thorax:** Same as the abdomen
**Wing Case:** Pheasant-tail fibers (same fibers that make the back and tails)

**Notes:** Bind the back and tail fibers atop the shank at the front of the abdomen, pull the tips of the fibers down, wind the wire around the shank and into the dubbing and then over the pheasant tips to bind them lightly. Tug half the tips firmly out to each side, tighten the wire to firm (really tight wire will weaken the fibers), and continue the wire forward as ribs. Don't cut the wire after making the ribs and binding the pheasant tips. Dub the thorax. Wind the hackle back over the thorax in three or four spirals, and then wind the wire forward through the turns of hackle to greatly toughen them. Unconventional to tie, Skip Nymphs have caught me trout all over North America and overseas.

## GABRIEL'S TRUMPET, GOLD

*Skip Morris*

**Hook:** #10-16 heavy wire, curved shank (scud/pupa style)
**Bead:** Gold metal
**Weight:** 0.015-inch lead or lead-substitute wire
**Thread:** Gold or yellow 8/0 or 6/0
**Tails:** Gold, amber, or yellow goose biots
**Rib:** Red copper wire
**Abdomen:** Gold Flashabou
**Wing Case:** Mottled-brown turkey primary
**Thorax:** Tan ostrich herl
**Hackle:** One ginger, gold, or tan hen-neck hackle

**Notes:** You can use larger diameter lead-substitute wire for the largest hook sizes. Wind the herl back for the thorax, bind its end with a few tight turns of the thread, and then spiral the thread forward through the herl to toughen it. Wind the hackle as a short collar behind the bead, and trim it on top or part it down the sides before pulling the wing case over the top.

More patterns for winter trout rivers (clockwise from top): Gulper Special, Griffith's Gnat, and Black Ghost. SKIP MORRIS

## GULPER SPECIAL

*Al Troth*

**Hook:**       #12-22 light wire, standard length to 1X long
**Thread:**     8/0 or 6/0 in a color to blend with the body
**Parachute Wing:** Poly yarn in white, orange, yellow, or chartreuse (whatever color you can best see)
**Parachute Hackle:** Any reasonable mayfly color
**Tail:**       Hackle fibers, same color as the hackle
**Body:**       Synthetic dubbing

## GRIFFITH'S GNAT

*George Griffith*

**Hook:**       #18-26 light wire, short to standard length
**Thread:**     Olive, gray, or black 8/0 or finer
**Hackle:**     One, grizzly, spiraled up the body
**Body:**       Peacock herl

## BLACK GHOST

**Hook:**       #6-10 heavy wire, 4X to 6X long
**Thread:**     Black 8/0, 6/0, or 3/0
**Tail:**       Dyed-yellow hackle fibers
**Rib:**        Flat silver tinsel, thin to medium
**Body:**       Black floss
**Throat:**     Yellow hackle fibers
**Wing:**       Four white saddle hackles, in two sets, the sets cupped together

*Rick Hafele*

# Name That Hatch
## Improve Your Bug ID Skill without Getting a Degree in Entomology

O ne of the more confusing aspects of fly fishing for trout is identifying the specific insect or "hatch" that trout are taking. Of course one first has to decide that being able to put a name on a bug is worthwhile to begin with. Maybe yes, maybe no.

# Rick Hafele

## Nymph or Larva?

These two terms can be rather confusing. Technically speaking, "nymph" refers to the juvenile stage of insects without a pupa stage, while "larva" refers to the juvenile stage of insects with a pupa stage.

In fly fishing, "nymph" generally refers to the underwater stage of any insect, and to the patterns that imitate them. ■

By this I mean that knowing the name of a hatch won't necessarily help you catch more trout. If you get a good look at what's on the water—see its size and shape, and watch its behavior and how fish are feeding on it—then you should be able to select an appropriate pattern, know how to present it, and in the process fool plenty of trout. So why bother with the whole problem of knowing what to call it? Several reasons come to mind.

First, let's say that for some unknown reason you didn't fool any trout during a hatch, even though you saw it up close and selected an appropriate pattern. This means that either your pattern or your presentation, or both, weren't right. So when you get home you decide to figure this out. What have others done during this hatch to catch trout? What patterns do they recommend and how do they fish them? But wait, how can you track down this information without knowing the name of the insect? Well, you can't. Maybe you'll get lucky and see a photo in a book or on the web, or hear someone else talking about the same hatch and give it a name (but is it the right name?), or maybe you'll just guess and figure close is close enough.

Second, maybe you do catch a bunch of trout during a certain hatch. Now you want to share your success with others and explain the pattern and tactic you used. Once again you will need to give the insect on the water a name in order to let others know what your fly was imitating so they can be prepared when they run into the same insect. And maybe you came up with a new pattern that worked extremely well and you want to explain to others how it's the perfect fly for the hatch. Oh, darn, now what was that insect?

Last, what if there is no hatch and no feeding trout and you want to figure out what fly might be good to use. Remembering that all you need to do to get some idea about what the trout are eating is pick up a few rocks from a riffle and see what nymphs are most abundant, you stoop over and lift a nice cobble from the stream. Hmm . . . there are many different kinds of nymphs running around. Which one is most likely ending up in the trout's stomach? And then you remember that mayfly swimming nymphs are really important to imitate when present. But what do they look like and how can you tell them apart from the other nymphs?

All three of these scenarios present situations where knowing how to recognize different insects would be quite useful. But there's one more reason I'm going to give that has nothing to do with usefulness at all. This reason is just about enjoying your day more by really understanding and appreciating the diversity of life found in streams and lakes. When it comes to richness of life, streams and lakes are quite remarkable. There's as much or more diversity and drama on the bottom of a stream as there is on an African savanna. And when it comes to unusual adaptations and behavior, I can't imagine a place with more unusual approaches to life than some of the insects found in streams and lakes. But without some knowledge of who's who, it's like walking through a tropical jungle without knowing any birds.

So I'm not saying you need to get better at recognizing different insects, but if you think you'd like to, then what follows are some ideas that will help you improve your hatch identification skills.

## Getting Started

One of the big challenges with learning to recognize all the important hatches is a direct result of their incredible diversity. The actual variety of aquatic insect species numbers in the thousands. So, to begin with, our goal is not to become entomologists who can identify everything they see to species. Not even entomologists can manage that. To become an expert taxonomist one has to specialize in just one order, family, or even a single genus of insect. The result of this amazing, but confusing, diversity is that fly fishers actually lump numerous species together when naming a specific hatch.

The Blue-Winged Olive, or BWO, mayfly hatch is an excellent example. The BWO common name refers to the abundant and important mayflies in the family Baetidae, and usually the genus *Baetis*. But there are other genera of Baetidae that are called Blue-Winged Olives as well, such as *Diphetor* and *Acentrella*, to name just two. The number of species within all the possible genera adds up to well over fifty. Therefore, when a fly fisher finds a Blue-Winged Olive hatch in progress it could be one of more than fifty different species, and there's really no way for the fly fisher to know which one. No wonder dozens of fly patterns in different sizes and colors could be needed when trying to imitate BWOs.

Many anglers are unaware of this lack of accuracy when it comes to naming insect hatches and become frustrated that they can't be more specific. The reality however, is that for all but a few hatches that are comprised of a single species (*Pteronarcys californica* for the Salmonfly hatch, for example), nearly all hatches referred to by anglers consist of multiple species that can't be easily distinguished, even by trained entomologists. On the plus side, understanding this level of diversity will help you understand why the BWO dun pattern you used last week on Beaver Creek doesn't match the BWO dun you see on the water today only 10 miles away on Rock Creek.

Learning to recognize the important hatches also means becoming familiar with both the underwater nymphal and larval stages as well as the terrestrial winged adult stages. No small task. So take your time and don't expect to figure this out over night. As they say—enjoy the process!

# Step 1
## Know the Orders

If you aren't able to quickly recognize the underwater and adult stages of each of the major orders of aquatic insects, that's where you should start. Here's a list of those orders:

Mayflies—Ephemeroptera
Stoneflies—Plecoptera
Caddisflies—Trichoptera
True Flies—Diptera
Dragonflies and Damselflies—Odonata
Backswimmers and Water boatmen—Hemiptera
Alderflies and Hellgrammites—Megaloptera
Aquatic Moths—Lepidoptera
Beetles—Coleoptera

You can prioritize your efforts by focusing on mayflies, stoneflies, caddisflies, and Diptera. These four orders produce 90 percent or more of the hatches fly fishers need to know. The following table summarizes the characteristics of these four orders for nymphs/larvae and adults.

# Step 2
## Learn the key groups in each of the four major orders

Once you are able to quickly recognize the orders of insects in both the underwater and adult stages, you are ready to take the next step. Because of the huge diversity of insects in each of the four major orders, it's not reasonable to try to learn all the hatches at once. A better approach is to learn key groups of hatches within each order. I've included a breakdown of these groups for the four major orders in the following tables. As you go through these groups, the two most important characteristics to pay attention to are tails (number and length) and gills (number, shape, and location).

# Step 3
## Get some good reference books on aquatic insect identification

I suspect this is more than enough to digest in one sitting. Look carefully at the photos and listed characteristics until you feel like you have a good sense of each subgroup within each order. To get to the next level in hatch identification, you will be well served by reading some of the excellent books that discuss insect hatches. Quite a few books have been written and illustrated for the fly fisher on this very topic. Some that I consider to be well worth your time if you wish to really get proficient at hatch identification are on page 209. Some of these books fit easily into your fishing vest, others will work best at home

# *Rick Hafele*

## Major Order ID Traits

| Order | Nymph/Larva Characteristics | Adult Characteristics |
|---|---|---|
| **Mayflies** | Mayfly nymph. RICK HAFELE **Tails:** 3, though a few species have only 2. **Gills:** Gills of various shapes and sizes always found on 3 to 7 abdominal segments. **Legs:** 6. **Wing pads:** Dark brown to black wing pads present on mature nymphs. Two pairs generally present, but only one pair visible. **Antennae:** Present but small and inconspicuous. | Mayfly adult. RICK HAFELE **Tails:** 2 or 3 depending on species. **Wings:** Generally 4 with the hind wings half or less the size of front wings; some species with only 2 wings. **Wing position:** Wings can't fold back flat on top of abdomen—stand straight up or straight out to each side. **Flight:** Generally moderately fast to slow erratic up-and-down flight. |
| **Stoneflies** | Stonefly nymph. RICK HAFELE **Tails:** 2. **Gills:** Short, slender, fingerlike gills found on the underside of the thorax and/or head. Many species with no visible gills. **Legs:** 6. **Wing pads:** 2 pairs of dark brown to black wing pads present on mature nymphs. **Antennae:** 2 long, well-developed antennae present. | Stonefly adult. RICK HAFELE **Tails:** 2, though they vary greatly in length depending on species. **Wings:** 4 wings of nearly equal size present on most species. Adults of a few species lack wings, or have short non-functional wings. **Wing position:** Wings lie flat on top of abdomen when not flying. **Flight:** Generally fly slow and relatively straight. Wings often beat slow enough to see wings in flight. |

PHOTOS BY RICK HAFELE

## Major Order ID Traits

| Order | Nymph/Larva Characteristics | Adult Characteristics |
|-------|------------------------------|------------------------|
| **Caddisflies** | Caddis Larva. RICK HAFELE | Caddis adult. RICK HAFELE |

**Caddisflies — Nymph/Larva Characteristics**

**Tails:** None—tip of abdomen with two small anal hooks.
Larvae of most species build portable cases out of many different materials.
**Gills:** Present or absent. When present they are slender, fingerlike filaments on various abdominal segments.
**Legs:** 6.
Wingpads: None.
**Antennae:** 2, but they are so small they can't be seen without a microscope.

**Caddisflies — Adult Characteristics**

**Tails:** None.
**Wings:** 4 with front and hind wings of nearly equal size, though hind wings usually a little larger.
**Wing position:** Wings fold up in inverted V or tent shape when not flying.
**Flight:** Generally moderately fast to fast with very erratic motion both up-and-down and side-to-side.

**Diptera**

Diptera larva. RICK HAFELE

Diptera adult. RICK HAFELE

**Diptera — Nymph/Larva Characteristics**

**Tails:** None.
**Gills:** Often none, but can also be slender filaments in various locations.
**Legs:** None.
**Wing pads:** None.
**Antennae:** Usually 2, but often too small to see.
**Head:** Often greatly reduced and not visible or hidden inside thorax.

**Diptera — Adult Characteristics**

**Wings:** 2 only. Hind wings have become short clubbed stalks called "halteres."
**Wing position:** Wings held out to sides or flat on top of abdomen when not in flight.
**Flight:** Wide range of habits. Most fly moderately fast and in a rather straight line.

PHOTOS BY RICK HAFELE

# Rick Hafele

## Mayflies

| Group | Nymphs | Adults | Major Hatches |
|---|---|---|---|
| **Swimmers** | Mayfly swimmer nymph.<br><br>• Bodies very streamlined or torpedo-shaped.<br>• 2 or 3 tails, middle tail often shorter than 2 outer tails, or equal in length and fringed with fine hairs.<br>• Gills on abdominal segments 1–7 and usually oval-shaped.<br>• Moderate to very small in size (12s–22s). | Mayfly swimmer adult.<br><br>• Hind wings very small or absent in small species, a third the size of front wings in moderately large species.<br>• 2 tails.<br>• Color variable—usually gray, brown, or olive.<br>• Moderate to very small in size (12s–22s). | • Blue-Winged Olives.<br>• Speckle Winged Quills.<br>• Brown Duns.<br>• Black and Gray Drakes. |
| **Crawlers** | Mayfly crawler nymph.<br><br>• Bodies somewhat rectangular in shape, not torpedo shaped, and sometimes quite stout with spines.<br>• 3 tails equal in length with or without fringe of fine hairs.<br>• Gills variable, often just on abdominal segments 3–7 or 4–7. | Mayfly crawler adult.<br><br>• Hind wings absent on Tricos, otherwise about a third the size of front wings.<br>• 3 tails.<br>• Vary widely in size (10s–24s).<br>• Vary widely in color. | • Western Green Drakes.<br>• Flavs.<br>• Tricos.<br>• Mahogany Duns.<br>• Sulphurs.<br>• Hendrickson/Red Quill. |

PHOTOS BY RICK HAFELE

# Mayflies

| Group | Nymphs | Adults | Major Hatches |
|---|---|---|---|
| **Clingers** | Mayfly clinger nymph. <br><br>• Bodies flat, eyes on top of head, and head widest part of body. <br>• 2 or 3 tails, though most species with 3. <br>• Gills on abdominal segments 1–7 and typically large, oval platelike in shape. | Mayfly clinger adult. <br><br>• Hind wings present and typically about a third the size of front wings. <br>• Head retains flattened appearance of nymphs. <br>• 2 tails. <br>• Size typically 12s–16s. <br>• Vary widely in color, but most often brown to light tan. | • Quill Gordon. <br>• Light Cahill. <br>• American March Brown. <br>• Western March Brown. <br>• Little Yellow May. |
| **Burrowers** | Mayfly burrower nymph. <br><br>• Bodies large, and tapered. <br>• 3 tails fringed with fine hairs. <br>• Large feather-like gills. <br>• Front of head with tusklike mandibles. | Mayfly burrower adult. <br><br>• Hind wings $\frac{1}{3}$ to almost $\frac{1}{2}$ size of front wings. <br>• Two or three tails <br>• Very large—6s–10s. | • Hex. <br>• Eastern Green Drake. <br>• Brown Drake. <br>• Yellow Drake. |

# Stoneflies

| Group | Nymphs | Adults | Major Hatches |
|---|---|---|---|
| **Little Brown Stones** |  Little Brown Stone nymph.  <br><br>• Generally small stoneflies with light to dark brown bodies (size 14s–18s). <br>• 2 tails length of abdomen. <br>• Gills present or absent. When present appear as single small filaments near base of legs or under head. <br>• Well developed antennae. |  Little Brown Stone adult.  <br><br>• Relatively small sized stoneflies from size 14s to 18s. <br>• Bodies light brown to black. <br>• Wings light gray, often with dark markings. Some species without wings. <br>• 2 tails range in length from almost too short to see to length of abdomen. | • Winter Stones. <br>• Little Brown Stones. <br><br>**Note:** Many species hatch during the winter and thus are called the winter stoneflies. Other species emerge in early spring to late fall. |
| **Yellow Stones** |  Yellow Stone nymph.  <br><br>• Small to moderate size stoneflies (size 10s to 16s). <br>• Bodies pale yellow to light brown, usually with distinct dark markings on thorax and abdomen. <br>• 2 tails the length of abdomen. <br>• Gills present or absent. Consist of small single filaments at base of legs or underside of head when present. |  Yellow Stone adult.  <br><br>• Moderate to small stoneflies in size 10s to 16s. <br>• Bodies pale to bright yellow (Yellow Sallies), or light to dark brown (Brown Willow flies). <br>• 2 tails roughly length of abdomen. <br>• 4 wings, though wings may be significantly reduced in some species. <br>• Body often with dark markings on thorax and abdomen. | • Yellow Sally. <br>• Brown Willow Flies or *Skwala*. <br><br>**Note:** Brown Willow Flies are the larger stones in this group and typically emerge in the spring. Yellow Sallies are fairly small and mostly emerge in the summer. |

PHOTOS BY RICK HAFELE

## Stoneflies

| Group | Nymphs | Adults | Major Hatches |
|---|---|---|---|
| **Golden Stones** |

Golden Stone nymph.

• Moderate to large stoneflies in sizes 6s–10s.
• Gills form clusters of slender filaments at base of legs.
• 2 tails the length of abdomen.
• Bodies light tan to dark brown with distinct marking on upper surface. |

Golden Stone adults.

• Moderate to large stoneflies with golden brown bodies (size 6s–10s).
• 2 tails length of abdomen.
• 4 wings. One species (*Claassenia sabulosa*) with greatly reduced wings. | • Golden Stones.

**Note:** Nymphs require 2 to 3 years to reach maturity and thus many immature nymphs are small in size (12s–14s), and outnumber large mature nymphs. |
| **Giant Stones or Salmonflies** |

Salmonfly nymph.

• Large stoneflies in sizes 4s to 8s when mature.
• Gills form clusters of slender filaments along underside of thorax and first 2 or 3 abdominal segments.
• 2 tails much shorter than abdomen.
• Bodies light brown to black without dark markings. |

Salmonfly adult.

• Large stoneflies (size 4s to 8s).
• Bodies brown on top and orange underneath.
• 4 large gray wings. | • Salmonfly.

**Note:** Nymphs require 3 to 4 years to reach maturity and thus many immature nymphs are small in size (12s–14s), and outnumber large mature nymphs. |

# Rick Hafele

## Caddisflies

| Group | Larvae | Adults | Major Hatches |
|---|---|---|---|
| **Free-living Caddis** | Free-living Caddis larva.<br><br>• Moderate sized caddis—10s to 14s.<br>• Bodies dark olive to bright green.<br>• No tails, but with well-developed anal hooks.<br>• Gills absent or present. Single filaments on abdomen when present.<br>• Do not build a case or shelter. | Free-living Caddis adult.<br><br>• Moderately large, size 10s to 14s.<br>• Bodies olive to green.<br>• Wings mottled gray.<br>• Antennae roughly body length. | • Green Rock Worm.<br><br>**Note:** 100+ species in North America. |
| **Net-spinning Caddis** | Net-spinning Caddis larva.<br><br>• Moderate to small caddis—12s to 16s.<br>• Bodies range from tan to dark brown to olive to dark green.<br>• Do not build a portable case, but attach spiderlike web of silk on sides of stones in riffles.<br>• Gills are clusters of slender filaments along underside of abdomen.<br>• Well-developed anal hooks. | Net-spinning Caddis adult.<br><br>• Moderate to small, size 12s to 16s.<br>• Bodies tan to brown.<br>• Wings light tan to brown with light spotting.<br>• Antennae roughly body length. | • Spotted Sedge.<br>• Little Sister Sedge. |

PHOTOS BY RICK HAFELE

Rick Hafele

## Caddisflies

| Group | Larvae | Adults | Major Hatches |
|---|---|---|---|
| **Case-building Caddis** | Case-building Caddis larva.<br><br>• Larvae construct portable tubelike cases made out of large variety of materials and shapes.<br>• Wide range of sizes, from 6s to 22s.<br>• Body color varies. | Case-building Caddis adult.<br><br>• Wide range of sizes and colors.<br>• 4 wings of variable color.<br>• Antennae one to three times body length. | • Saddle-Case Caddis.<br>• October Caddis.<br>• American Grannom.<br>• Mother's Day Caddis.<br>• Dark Blue Sedge.<br>• Long-Horned Sedge.<br>• and more! |

PHOTOS BY RICK HAFELE

# Rick Hafele

## Diptera

| Group | Larvae | Adults | Major Hatches |
|---|---|---|---|
| **Midges/ Chironomids** | Midge larva. RICK HAFELE<br><br>• Body varies in size from moderate to tiny: 12s to 30s.<br>• Distinct head capsule.<br>• No legs or fleshy prolegs.<br>• No tails.<br>• Gills small; single filaments near head and tip of abdomen, sometimes absent. | Midge adult. DAVE HUGHES<br><br>• Body in many colors and sizes, but generally small (12s–30s).<br>• 2 front wings. Hind wings appear as small, clubbed stalks called "halteres."<br>• Wing shorter than abdomen.<br>• Do not bite. | • Midge or chironomid.<br><br>**Note:** There are literally thousands of species of this group in streams and lakes. Just learn to recognize main group—midges— and then observe color and size. |
| **Crane flies** | Crane fly larva. RICK HAFELE<br><br>• Large to moderate size, 8s to 14s.<br>• Light tan to dark brown, tubular-looking larvae.<br>• Head hidden inside first thoracic segment.<br>• No thoracic legs, but short "prolegs" may be present on abdomen. | Crane fly adult. CAROL ANN MORRIS<br><br>• Large to moderate in size, 8s to 14s.<br>• Long legs.<br>• 2 wings: Front pair roughly body length. No hind wings; knobbed "halteres" instead. | • Crane flies.<br>• Mosquito hawks.<br>• Don't bite. |

PHOTOS BY RICK HAFELE

Will knowing the name of the mayfly on the water help you catch that big brown? Yes and no. But it will help you understand why you did or didn't and also help you enjoy the day that much more. RICK HAFELE

or in your vehicle. Because of the large diversity of hatches, many of these books are regional in scope, which makes them less confusing and more useful when fishing in the region covered. This list is by no means complete, so I apologize to those I have not included.

## Books

Dave Hughes. *Pocketguide to Western Hatches*. Stackpole Books, 2011. Dave's new book. Check it out!

Dave Hughes and Rick Hafele. *Western Mayfly Hatches*. Frank Amato Publications, 2004.

Rick Hafele and Scott Roederer. *An Angler's Guide to Aquatic Insects and Their Imitations*. Johnson Books, 1995.

Arlen Thomason. *BugWater*. Stackpole Books, 2010.

Thomas Ames Jr. *Hatch Guide for New England Streams*. Frank Amato Publications, 2000.

Thomas Ames Jr. *Caddisflies: A Guide to Eastern Species for Anglers and Other Naturalists*. Stackpole Books, 2009.

Thomas Ames Jr. *Fishbugs: The Aquatic Insects of an Eastern Fly Fisher*. Countryman Press, 2005.

Jim Schollmeyer. *Hatch Guide for Lakes*. Frank Amato Publications, 1995.

Carl Richards and Bob Braendle. *Caddis Super Hatches*. Frank Amato Publications, 1997.

Patrick McCafferty. *Aquatic Entomology*. Science Books International, 1981.

And if you find that you just can't get enough about identifying aquatic insects, then you may want to get the volume used by many aquatic entomologists:

R. W. Merritt, K. W. Cummins, and M. B. Berg (editors). *An Introduction to the Aquatic Insects of North America* Fourth edition. Kendall Hunt Publishing, 2008.

The late Sylvester Nemes, author of one of my favorite fishing books, *The Soft-Hackled Fly*, plays a fish that took an expertly fished soft-hackle on the swing through a riffle on the Yellowstone River in Montana. DAVE HUGHES

Dave Hughes

# Favorite Fishing Books
## Small Is Better

I have a small set of five fishing books that have always been right up there toward the top on my list of favorites to pull off the shelf, reread, mull over for any new considerations I might get out of them, and once again put them to use at both my tying vise and out on streams and sometimes stillwaters. "Small" is the defining term for these books: Each is minor in size, short in word count, easily read in a day, magically applicable to water after only an evening or two spent at the bench. I suspect I've read each of them at least three or four times. I'm sure that if Clotho spins her thread a bit longer, and Atropos refrains from snipping it, I'll read each more than once again. That is not, by the way, fly-tying thread that I'm talking about.

# Dave Hughes

A common condition, beyond their size, runs through all of these books. Each is tightly focused on a single, narrow aspect of fly fishing, and each treats its chosen subject extraordinarily well. They all offer beautiful treatments, which is not to say that all are written beautifully, or in some cases even written well. But they all inspire. Any time I pick up and reread any part of any one of these books, I'm ignited with the desire to take the short hike to my vise, to tie a few of the flies about which it is written. Beyond that, and perhaps much more importantly, I'm then propelled out toward some trout stream or lake or pond on which I can fish these flies.

The following books are discussed in the approximate order to which I was exposed to them, not necessarily in the order in which they were written and published. For most of them, I have two and sometimes three editions on my shelves. I'll take note of my favorite of those.

*The Art of Tying the Wet Fly & Fishing the Flymph* by James E. Leisenring and Vernon S. "Pete" Hidy. First published in 1941, only the second edition, released in 1971, included the material on the flymph. My dad had only three fly-fishing books on his shelves when I grew up; one of them was a copy of the first 1941 edition of this Leisenring and Hidy book. Much later in life, Rick Hafele and I were giving one of our early "Entomology and the Artificial Fly" workshops in Boise, Idaho. Pete Hidy slipped into the back of the room and spoke quietly with each of us while the other was up front pontificating.

That weekend Pete invited us to his house, demonstrated on his kitchen table how to tie flymphs in his manner, gave each of us a flymph-tying kit, including a body-spinning block he'd constructed by hand. I'll always remember that he led us downstairs to the basement, where he had a slide projector set up. He sat the two of us in wicker chairs, one on each side of the projector, then stood behind it and presented an hour-long private slide show on tying and fishing flymphs.

The subject of the book is wet flies, a few of them what we now call soft hackles, a few more traditional winged wets, but most of them wingless wets, which after Pete Hidy coined the term, are now referred to more commonly as flymphs. The focus of the book is how to tie wet flies so they ". . . become alive in the eyes of the trout." Instructions include how to spin

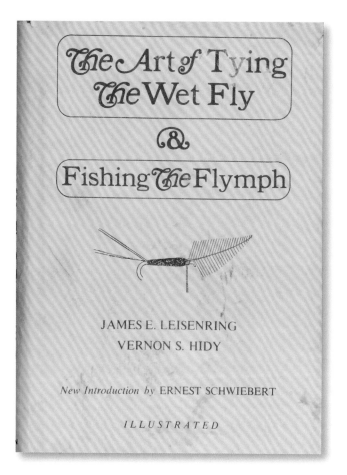

bodies on separate silks, so the color of the thread percolates through the outer color of the fur when the fly becomes wet, which a wet fly often does when you apply it against trout.

The book is short, its word count small, each of those words carefully chosen to fit its subject. It is illustrated with black-and-white photos and line drawings of a quality that would not cut it today, though they adequately drive home all points being made. Surprisingly, few of those points are about fishing the flies you'll learn to tie from the book. Only a single tactic, the well-known Leisenring Lift, is recorded. Pete told Rick and me that the two of them planned to follow the first book with a second focused on tactics to fish their wet flies. The first book was subsumed by a war in which we became highly involved in its year of publication, and the second book was never written. Its absence is one of fly fishing's tragedies. Pete told us that the Leisenring Lift was one of the minor tactics Jim Leisenring, the master, used in his own fishing.

What this book inspires its reader to do is collect the materials unique to tying wets—British land bird wings and capes, furs such as mole, peacock herl left in the sun to turn bronze—and to tie in the manner devised to make the flies look alive. You'll spin separate bodies and perhaps even build the simple spinning block with which to make those lifelike bodies. You'll be inspired, as well, to hurry out and fish the flies, though you'll not be instructed as well as you'd wish in how to do it. I wrote about a tactic called the Hidy Subsurface Swing in my book *Wet Flies*; the same technique is covered in Ed Engle's fine new book *Trout Lessons*. That and the famous Leisenring Lift can be added to standard wet-fly tactics and Jock Scott and A. H. E. Wood's greased line technique to help you develop a full range of wet-fly tactics.

My favorite edition of *The Art of Tying the Wet Fly & Fishing the Flymph* is the 1971 Crown printing published by Nick Lyons. Some consideration was given by Stackpole, a few years ago, to bring the book out in a new edition—I was to write the introduction—but the market was deemed too small, based on my own judgment, which might have been faulty. The book is not currently in print. One site on the net lists eleven used copies available, from $54.25. So it's out there, if you'd like to be inspired to tie flymphs right from the source.

*New Streamside Guide to Naturals and Their Imitations* by Art Flick. First published in 1947, with a second edition released in 1969, and subsequent editions still in print. I came across this book in the 1969 edition shortly after my return from a dustup in Southeast Asia. I was just getting back to fly fishing, and it was my first exposure to the concept of matching hatches . . . *Western Hatches* was ten years into the future at that point, and so little was available on insects in the West that it made sense to interpret from this little book about insects and imitations in the East.

The tight focus of the book is on a few of the most important Eastern hatches, almost all mayflies, almost all somewhat large, almost all imitated with traditional hackled Catskill dressings, many of them over-hackled in the spider style. Flick is said to have quit fishing for a season or two; he carried his rod so he wouldn't look like a mad man out thrashing around with a butterfly net—you should see Rick out there on streams sometimes!—but he collected all the major hatches on his single home stream, the Esopus in upstate New York. He tied beautiful flies to match them. Imitations are always shaped by tradition and

by water: Flick's traditions were those Catskill ties, and the water of the Esopus was brisk, so the hackled dressings were perhaps necessary.

Such high-floating dry-fly dressings were ideal for the small Oregon streams on which I spent most of my time in those days. Not surprisingly, it was not difficult to find counterparts to those Eastern insects in our Western hatches, and even less surprisingly, those bushy ties worked as well out here as they did in the East. They were for a different set of insects, in taxonomic terms, but trout in those days lacked microscopes and advanced degrees in entomology . . . some think those things are still true about trout.

The main thing the *Streamside Guide* did, in my own fishing, was open my eyes to the wise idea to collect what the trout were eating and to fish flies that looked at least a little like the naturals. Flick's focus and philosophy were refreshing, at a time when I was frantically trying to capture every insect, and tie a separate imitation for each: "The better fly-tyers will realize they have more to gain than to lose in a reduction of the number of patterns, for they know that many of those now tied could very easily be eliminated." That fact has been multiplied many times since Art Flick wrote it, and the body of flies invented for trout has burst the dam, flooded the landscape.

Flick's treatment was spare, direct, unadorned with stories. Every word stuck to its point that you should collect a natural, parse out its primary parts, tie an imitation that looked a lot like it and floated on the water where you intended to apply it. It's a formula that works East, West, and everywhere in between. The book is illustrated with a few line drawings of the naturals, plus center-page color plates of the most important insects and the flies that imitate them.

Flick's *Streamside Guide* is still an exceptional read and very cogent for those who fish hatches in the East. In the minor amount of collecting and fishing I've done there, I've encountered several of the species Flick listed. Modern patterns tend more toward exact imitation, with collar-hackled flies not nearly as common as they once were. It would be an interesting assignment, however, to tie a set of his flies, use them in appropriate circumstances, and see if they might not work as well as, perhaps even better than, more modern ties.

If you fish the West, then the book is more a prescription for observing your own hatches, finding—or inventing your own—dressings to match them. The book inspired me, when I first encountered it, to tie Flick's flies, go out, and find hatches over which to fish them. It still inspires me at times to tie his gorgeous and graceful flies, to fish them on small streams, where they still work fine. But I am more inspired by the book to do my own research, to discover my own hatches, to tie flies that match them, and in the manner of Art Flick, once he got his research behind him, to go out and fish them.

My favorite edition of the book is the 1969 Crown hardbound. I also own a Winchester Press/Nick Lyons Books softbound from a later printing, and I believe the book has remained in print in one form or another almost continually. One site listed four used hardbounds from $39.98.

*Tying and Fishing the Fuzzy Nymphs* by E. H. "Polly" Rosborough. First published privately in 1965, then as a booklet by Orvis in 1969, and finally by Stackpole Books in 1978. I found the book first in this late printing. Orvis at that time was featuring Polly's full set of nymphs in their catalog. I cut the plates out of

the catalog and taped them to the frontspiece of my copy of the book, giving me far better photos of each fly than the book itself held. I'm glad I did that; Orvis subsequently dropped most of the flies, and therefore the pictures, so you would be unable to find them now unless you could come up with an ancient Orvis catalog . . . which would probably be too valuable to cut up for its fly plates.

The subject of Polly's classic book, as its title describes it, is his unique fuzzy nymphs. He adhered tightly to it, describing how he originated them, how he tied them, how he roughed them up, and how he fished them. It's a thorough treatment, in his unusual "Polly the Parrot" voice, less well-written than well-spoken. But you'll have no trouble extracting any of his meaning, and you'll enjoy every moment you spend on it.

It's more than interesting to note that Polly's flies are neither tied nor fished by many folks so few years after the publication of his book. The reasons are fairly simple. Polly fished a rare set of waters in southern Oregon and northern California. They were, and still are, low-gradient waters, with mostly spring origins, and heavy populations of large swimmer mayflies, stoneflies, and caddis. As a consequence, Polly's imitations were tied on long shank hooks, size 12 and up for the most part, and though they are nymphs in theory, they're best when fished more like streamers in reality.

Polly never weighted his nymphs and did not tie them often in small sizes. I violated a couple of his rules to take the largest redside rainbow I've caught to date on the Deschutes. I tied his Muskrat, usually a size 10 or 12 nymph, on a size 18 hook and weighted it slightly. I fished it as the trailer behind a Salmonfly nymph, hooked a trout with which I had to be quite gentle, and brought it in after a long fight at the edges of a brutal riffle. The trout turned out to be hooked on the trailer; it was 20 inches long, shaped like a football, and must have weighed 4 pounds then, which has it up to around 6 pounds now, some years later, when I've learned to estimate trout sizes more accurately.

My copy of Polly's book has color plates on the end plates, not as useful as one would want today, but fine back in 1978. The few black-and-white photos and line drawings illustrate critical points, but it's fortunate that Polly's words—Polly's voice—describes quite well what you need to know to tie his flies.

Though you will not necessarily want to tie and fish all of Polly's nymphs, you should learn quite a bit from the descriptions of his tying techniques. The main thing you'll get out of the book, however, is separate from the flies, or even his techniques, unique as they were to his unusual set of waters. The larger lesson you can learn from Polly's book is the need to go out on your home waters, collect the nymphs trout feed on there, and tie your own set of flies to fish appropriately in the conditions you encounter. The true lesson from Polly Rosborough is his vision: his interpretation of naturals into fly patterns, and his application of tactics that worked where he fished those nymphs that looked more like streamers. What you see on your own waters will be different; what you tie to fish there will not be the same; the tactics you use will not be Polly's. But if you can see your own waters the way he saw his, tie your own set of imitations the way he did his, learn to fish your own flies on your own waters, you'll be applying Polly's lessons beyond any that you will ever get from more directly applicable books.

My favorite edition of *Tying and Fishing the Fuzzy Nymphs* is my 1978 Stackpole hardbound, with the codicil that it contains my Orvis catalog plates. You won't have an easy time finding those. The book has been in and out of print in other versions. A quick check of the net revealed a site with fifteen copies from $14.95. There is little reason not to own this book and thereby to be inspired by the lessons of Polly Rosborough.

*Fishing the Midge* by Ed Koch. First printed in 1972 by Freshet Press, this fine little book was released in a second edition by Stackpole Books in the 1990s. It is one of my favorite works because of its handy size, fine illustrations and photos, and instructive vignettes that take each of his creations out on a stream, shows how it was created. The best of fly-fishing writing is the kind in which the author takes you to the stream with him. Koch's is a rare one of that fine kind.

The subject of the book is midge flies, with the word being used in the sense of a small imitation—size 16 to 24—rather than the entomology meaning of the word midge: insects in the order Chironomidae. There are those, but there are also midge flies tied for small mayflies, caddis nymphs, scuds, sow

bugs, and anything else tiny. With this tight focus on small flies, the book has quite a broad range in the world of trout food forms.

Ed Koch's writing is among the best in the fly-fishing world, and his little stories will have you delving deeply into the origins of each of his fly patterns. He fished many of the most storied waters in the East: the Yellow Breeches, Letort, Falling Springs, Big Spring, and others where trout are as selective as they get. I spent a day walking the Letort near Carlisle, Pennsylvania, with Ed; it was enlightening in terms of seeing, on the ground, the visions that he'd created in my mind . . . but it was January, snow lay on the banks of the little spring creek, and we didn't even try to wet a line.

This book is illustrated with black-and-white photos of tying steps and the finished flies. The photos are among the best, in terms of showing detail, and Koch's step-by-step directions are as clear and simple as I've seen. It's part of what makes this book such a gem: tight focus, small flies, beautiful descriptions of both tying and fishing, and an aesthetic, thoughtful layout by the late Joan Stoliar, one of my favorite characters in all of fishing—designer of the lifesaving Folstaff and the little Fly Tyer's Carry All portable tying kit that I still have stashed away in a bottom drawer of my fly-tying desk. Joan designed most of the Freshet Press fly-fishing books of an earlier era, and all that she designed stood out as the best in their class. She was also a sweet lady, but she is another story.

The book has central color plates that show some, though not all, of the natural insects and their imitations. Like the black-and-white step-by-step photos, they're excellent.

This is a beautiful little book that you can put to your own use on trout streams to this day, especially if you fish spring creeks and tailwaters where trout are often selective to small naturals. It makes no difference that its emphasis is Eastern; with such small imitations, everything tends to become the same, all around the fly-fishing world. More than anything, it will inspire you to buy a small fly box, tie a set of Ed's small flies, and take them with you on your next trip to a stream.

My favorite edition of *Fishing the Midge* is the Freshet Press 1972 printing designed by Joan Stoliar. I found four copies listed from $14.95 on my favorite angling website. The Stackpole edition is just as good, if not quite so pretty.

*The Soft-Hackled Fly* by Sylvester Nemes. First released in 1975, published by the author, then kept in print by Stackpole Books, and recently rereleased with all the original material plus new chapters on tying tiny soft-hackles. I was drawn to the book immediately after it was published, in part because of my fascination with wet flies, in another large part because of my love for small books focused on single subjects.

Syl passed away in February of 2011; his book is the ultimate tight treatment of a very important aspect of fly fishing that had been overlooked in this country for many, many years. Though he is often criticized for not "inventing" soft-hackles, Syl never did make any claims in that direction and clearly credits Yorkshire border region originators of soft-hackled dressings. His beautiful little book did, however, bring these flies to the attention of American fly fishers, and they've been taking lots of trout, for those who fish them even casually, ever since.

I'll give you a recent example, though it's not the intent of this short review to step out on streams. I just got back from a trip to Arkansas, giving a

workshop for the great North Arkansas Fly Fisher's club in Mountain Home and the surrounding area. The day before the workshop, my host and club president Mike Tipton took me out to the Norfork of the White River to squeeze in a few hours fishing. While I rigged up with nymphs to fish a "shoal"—a riffle anywhere else—Mike tied on a size 12 March Brown Spider soft-hackle, right out of Syl's book by way of my book *Wet Flies*, and instantly began dancing trout. My nymphs, meanwhile, fished from the opposite side of the riffle, over what I presume was the same set of trout, went largely ignored. Until I made a switch, Mike out-fished me at a rate of about three to one.

I first met Sylvester, and his fine book, in an interesting way. I read it, was captured by it, was enthused to tie a bunch of his soft-hackles, and thence propelled out to fish them. I did very well. I got permission to review the book for a magazine. In my review I quoted Syl as saying the flies and the method did not often catch big trout, that his largest on them was a 20-inch brown from the Madison in the park. The review prompted a somewhat indignant letter from Syl; he wanted me to know he'd just been on the Yellowstone and caught two trout over 20 inches long in one day. I reminded him that I'd only quoted him, and we became friends by correspondence for some years. Finally I sent my book to him and asked if he'd autograph it.

He did more than that. I'd tied each of his fourteen flies listed in the book and hooked them into the pages next to their dressings. It was a sort of desecration, but mine was a softbound, so I didn't mind reducing the value of the book. But Syl tied each of the flies and slipped his into the pages alongside mine. He labeled mine DH and his SH, and I now have a softbound copy of the book with the listed dressings all tied by me—mine look crude compared to his!—and by Syl. At the top of the same page, he wrote: "Dave, how'd you like to find this in an attic in 2054? Good luck till then. Syl." Neither Syl nor I will be around to know about it, but I do hope somebody finds this copy of the book in an attic at mid-century, and I also hope they know the value of what they've found.

I fished with Syl and his wonderful wife Hazel a few times in subsequent years, and there would be stories in that, but again the subject here is his book, and like his book, I ought to stick more tightly to my subject. His topic was soft-hackles: their origins, his

## Sources for Books

You can Google fly-fishing books and quickly come up with several sources for them, including the obvious Amazon, which dominates book sales to the point that little authors like me quail before them. But there are several specialty fishing booksellers—Jim Adams, Gary Estabrook, Judith Bowman, a few I hope I'll be forgiven for not having at the forefront of my brain at this moment. One that might not come up in your search is The Angler's Bookcase; Craig Douglass in New Mexico is one of my favorites. Be sure to track him down. ∎

introduction to them, his experiences with them, how to tie them, how to fish them. No book I've ever read has stuck as strictly to what it's about, nor has any ever written about its narrow subject so sparely and beautifully. Much of the beauty in Syl's prose is the way it fits its subject: very tight sentences describing a very simple subject.

The book has just a few black-and-white photos of the flies, and steps in tying them, as well as one color plate, showing the fourteen listed dressings, and some color shots of them working in the water. The photos are not overabundant, but they are adequate to show the process of getting a soft-hackle together. In truth, the photos are not needed; the pictures are in Syl's words.

This book has become perhaps my favorite fishing book of all time. I love getting it out, reading a chapter, tying a few flies, just for the pleasure of creating such beauty—those little soft-hackled wets, with their speckled partridge legs, look more alive than anything else you're likely to tie. Trout seem always to agree.

My favorite edition of the book is the 1975 Chatham Press printing, which I own in both hardbound and the softbound I've described. The new Stackpole edition has valuable information on tying small soft-hackles. A quick check of the web revealed thirteen used copies from $11.95. If you haven't read this small book, tied from it, and gone fishing with a bundle of enthusiasm afterward, I promise you've got a treat coming.

Skip Morris

# Winter Midges

If you don't know that midges are tiny, you don't know midges. They look like mosquitoes but are typically much smaller—ever seen a mosquito that would match a diminutive size 22 hook? Well 22 is no big deal for imitating a midge. So midges are easy to miss as they ride on their toes atop the surface of a river with their slivery, translucent dust-mote-size wings down at their sides. Many midges are dark and consequently all but disappear on dark water. So you really have to look to find them—which a lot of fly fishers don't, and consequently miss the hatch altogether. Get your head down close; watch the smooth surface of the lazy flows. If midges are there, you may see lots of them—midges like to hatch in mobs. That's what makes them, minuscule as they are, appealing to trout.

Patience is critical when watching the smooth, slow-moving parts of a river for signs of a midge hatch. Those signs include speck-size midges themselves of course, but also the softly expanding circles of trout sipping at the water's surface. Some fly fishers carry binoculars to see close-up just what the trout are doing and what's encouraging them to do it. CAROL ANN MORRIS

I've fished a lot of midge hatches, almost always during the cold months of October through March. So even though midges hatch year round (and I have fished midge hatches even in August), I tend to expect and look for them in winter and in the chilly weeks that border winter. Give me low water and hatching midges and sipping trout in November or February and I'll forget about numb toes and stinging hands. (Well, mostly . . . )

Trout know better than to waste a spoonful of energy on a pinch of protein, so trout's rises to midges are quiet dimples on the water. That's one good clue that midges are the main course. Still, close inspection of the surface is invaluable when it comes to identifying a midge hatch.

So just how small are the flies that imitate midges? A big one is size 18, and size 22 is probably average, but that's just the start—there are hooks for midge flies of size 24, 26, 28 . . . at certain times in certain places, even these are too large. Midges can get silly small. Once, among a few Colorado guides waiting for their clients, I plucked a midge off the edge of water

where trout were feeding. I commented on how diminutive the insect was and a guide who'd seen that hatch many times said, "Probably take a number 32 to match that . . . or smaller." He was right. Still, on rose the trout, some of them 3-pounders. I actually hooked a couple of the 3-pounders on size 26 midges tied short and 8X tippet. That got interesting fast.

A real midge hatch, the kind in which the insects are all over the water, is the height of fishing fine. You select your fish, watch it work, time its rises, cast upstream with slack to allow a long natural drift of the fly . . . But it's not always about working a specific fish. I've seen midge hatches bring trout up in clusters to pick steadily at the drift. When trout are working that close together you really can't single one out, but then, you don't need to. The trick then becomes working upstream through the fish, targeting the two or three lowest ones and, when one is hooked, guiding it quickly downstream before it spooks the feeders above it. The rising of trout is a powerful lure for the fly fisher, and a real midge hatch can be as good as that gets.

*Scan to watch Video:*
## Rigging for Midges

I can't imagine tippet heavier than 6X for midge dry flies and emergers of size 20 and smaller. With really tough trout in very clear water I'll go to 7X and, on occasion, 8X. I've seen 8X make the difference. But on most midge waters with flies of average midge size, 6X and 7X are all you'll need.

Tippet size runs differently for subsurface midge flies than for surface ones in my experience. That sunken tippet is harder for the trout to see than tippet that might be partially floating, and there's less light the deeper into the river a fly reaches. But theories aside, I normally go with 5X tippet for underwater midge flies, and the trout respond appropriately. In the clearest, laziest water, though, with smart trout . . . well, I'll go as fine on tippet as I feel I must. The trout will let me know just how fine that is.

Strategy for the deep midge fly is different too than for the floating one. When a hatch is on and the trout are nosing down identical midge adults and emergers on the water's surface or pupae just below the surface, you'd better catch a sample of the natural and match its length and probably its color with your flies. But the deep pupa or larva imitation isn't normally about hatches, so I just tie on whatever midge nymph looks right to me and toss it out there to see if it looks right to the trout.

When I fish a deep midge pupa fly, it's usually to fool very cautious trout that keep turning away from anything larger. I remember the jaded trout holding down in plain view in a small spring creek where the footpath from the parking lot first meets the water. Those trout were watched and worked on nearly all day every day. I tried a lot of nymphs only to see the fish drift to the side to let them pass . . . until I tried a size 20 pupa pattern as a dropper. Even with no hatch my tiny pupa pattern looked just fine, judging by the results. Difficult trout can be pushovers for little stuff even if it's not the littlest stuff—nymphs of size 18 and smaller just don't seem to arouse their suspicions the way a size 14 or 10 would.

My experience with midges has mostly been on tailwater rivers in Washington, Oregon, Idaho, and Colorado. Midges hatch in spring creeks and in freestone rivers fed right off the surface, and I fish such rivers every year, but for some reason not often during midge hatches.

**Below:** A throat pump revealed the variety of midge larvae and pupae this particular open-minded fish had taken. Even when trout aren't selective to a particular size or color or even stage of midge, they may still concentrate on midges. (I prefer the term "throat pump" to the common term "stomach pump"—the pump must be used gently and should reach in only to the base of a trout's throat, never into its stomach. A throat pump used roughly or with force becomes a tool of torture and death.) RICK HAFELE

# Skip Morris

The controlled volumes of tailwaters tend to collect the silt midges love. That may explain in part why such waters account for so much of my midge fishing. Spring creeks with their reliable flows tend to be silty, however, and slower freestone rivers can be silty, too.

Actually, it's not just tailwaters where I find most of my midge hatches but *low* tailwaters, to be precise. I don't recall fishing a midge hatch on a river above its normal height. So I asked my old friend, entomologist Rick Hafele, if midges prefer lower water for their hatching, and he said: "Never say never when it comes to bug behavior, so no, I wouldn't say that midges never hatch when the water is high. But, all things being equal, conditions for hatches and fishing will be much more favorable during low water than high. In the winter, high water often means colder water (not always though—never say never, remember), which will put at least a temporary hold on hatches in general, including midges. Trout will also be in a less active mood when the water is up."

Flat water, midges, rising trout—add fine tippets and skill to these elements and you have a shot at a magnificent day's fishing. RICK HAFELE

Midwinter midges tend to come off when the river has warmed to its maximum, which is normally early afternoon. As winter's cold slackens into early spring, midges may come off later in the day. Many times in the modest cool of fall I've caught trout well through a midday Blue-Winged Olive hatch and then switched to midge flies as the hatch changed over to midges, sometimes the midge fishing continuing right up until dark. But midges aren't big on fly fishers' rules; they hatch whenever they want.

It's the subtlety of midge hatches that probably appeals to me most, the trout nosing quietly amid the abundance of naturals, the lazy water—this is almost the antithesis of fishing the Salmonfly stonefly hatch (which, in its way, is just as satisfying as fishing midge hatches—thank God for variety!).

As with mayfly hatches, I go heavily to emergers and suspended nymphs during midge hatches. It's a fact of life that under most circumstances, a trout will prefer insects in some stage of sloughing off their shucks over fully hatched adults. That's because the emerging insect is half-stuck, wings still a crumple in that backpack of obsolete skin, legs partly trapped in the same now-frustrating sheath—in others words, the insect is easy pickings. It can't fly off or skitter away just as the trout reaches it as a fully emerged adult well might. The half-submerged, half-hatched insect is also easier to see below the mirrored underside of a river's surface than a midge adult standing atop, and on the far side of, that mirror.

For all of these reasons, midges that fail in their hatching, drifting awash in the surface, also appeal

## Scan to watch Video:
# Skip's Favorite Midge Patterns

greatly to trout. Fly fishers call such insects "cripples."

So I offer you one midge pupa pattern, one midge emerger pattern, and a cripple—all solid imitations.

For the pupa, the Disco Midge, Red (which is also commonly tied in pearl, olive, and, oddly, blue). It's a bright and simple midge pattern with a strong track record. It doesn't include a metal or glass bead, but you don't want a heavier bead-head fly if you need to drift a pupa just inches below the surface to a rising trout. You want just enough weight to get the fly submerged—with materials either absorbent or neutral in buoyancy the metal hook will take the fly under—but not so much weight that a little floatant smeared up the tippet to within a few inches of the fly won't support it.

Of course if you want to fish the pupa off a foot or less of tippet tied to the bend of a larger dry fly, a bead head is fine. Personally, I think that with angler-wise midge-sipping trout, the greased tippet is the way to go. Wise trout seem to eye that paired-up dry fly and pupa with suspicion. This all depends, of course, on how cagey your trout are.

But easily managed trout can grow wiser during midge hatches—it's baffling but true—at least in my fishing experience. While a midge or midge-size fly can fool a fussy trout even when there's no midge hatch, a hatch of midges does seem to turn even fairly willing trout cautious. I sometimes wonder if it isn't the casual sort of feeding that goes with tiny stuff that turns trout fussy—rather than rush greedily to a big caddisfly or stonefly and all that meat, the lazy rhythm of

midge feeding gives trout more time to consider each minuscule insect drifting near. The sluggish currents of midge water surely increase the trout's view of insects and flies, and the leisurely drift of both makes that view even clearer and longer.

For the emerging midge, I offer the good old Serendipity. It works. Rub a little floatant into the deer hair and let the fly drift drag-free. For the cripple, Smith's Black Cripple. Its intriguing wings of CDC offer stubborn buoyancy. Fish it as you would the Serendipity.

All three of these flies are—to my complete surprise!—among the hundreds in my book *Trout Flies for Rivers: Patterns from the West That Work Everywhere*. Not that I'm suggesting you purchase the book, you understand . . .

**Below:** A typical midge adult. Not a bad stand-in for a common mosquito—except that it takes a lot of average midges to equal the bulk of one average mosquito. DAVE HUGHES

# Skip Morris

## DISCO MIDGE, RED

**Hook:** #18-26 heavy to light wire, humped shank
**Thread:** Red 8/0
**Abdomen:** Red Krystal Flash or Accent Flash over a layer of the red working thread
**Thorax:** Peacock herl (or hare's mask dubbing or black thread)

## SERENDIPITY, GRAY

**Hook:** #14-22 light wire, humped shank (pupa/emerger hook)
**Thread:** Gray 8/0
**Body:** Gray Z-Lon or Antron yarn, twisted
**Head and Wing Case:** Deer hair

## SMITH'S BLACK CRIPPLE

*Todd Smith*

**Hook:** #18-24 light wire, humped shank (pupa/emerger hook)
**Thread:** Black 8/0
**Shuck:** One strand of Root Beer (light brown) Krystal Flash
**Abdomen:** Black Krystal Flash
**Wings:** White CDC
**Hackle:** Grizzly, spiraled over the thorax and trimmed flat underneath
**Thorax:** Fine buoyant black natural or synthetic dubbing

**Notes:** For the wing, hold a feather by its tip, stroke the fibers down the sides of the stem and hold them, bind the feather atop the shank as a wing, and trim off the tip of the feather. Make two such wings, parted. Interesting wing, eh? And a good one that's seldom seen.

# Index

Page numbers in italics indicate boxes, illustrations, photographs, and videos.